TAMPA THEATRE

University Press of Florida

Florida A&M University, Tallahassee / Florida Atlantic University, Boca Raton

Florida Gulf Coast University, Ft. Myers / Florida International University, Miami

Florida State University, Tallahassee / New College of Florida, Sarasota

University of Central Florida, Orlando / University of Florida, Gainesville

University of North Florida, Jacksonville / University of South Florida, Tampa

University of West Florida, Pensacola

Andrew T. Huse

TAMPA THEATRE

a century of stories

University Press of Florida
Gainesville / Tallahassee / Tampa / Boca Raton / Pensacola
Orlando / Miami / Jacksonville / Ft. Myers / Sarasota

Cover: Photo by Jeff Fay. Design by Mindy Basinger Hill.

Publication of this work is made possible by the generous members and donors of Tampa Theatre.

Published in the United States of America
Printed in Canada

31 30 29 28 27 26 6 5 4 3 2 1

LIBRARY OF CONGRESS CATALOGING-IN-PUBLICATION DATA

Names: Huse, Andrew T. author
Title: Tampa theatre : a century of stories / Andrew T. Huse.
Description: Gainesville : University Press of Florida, 2026. | Includes bibliographical references and index.
Identifiers: LCCN 2026010572 | ISBN 9780813079622 hardback
Subjects: LCSH: Tampa Theatre (Tampa, Fla.) | Motion picture theaters—Florida—Tampa—History | Historic buildings—Florida—Tampa | Historic preservation—Florida—Tampa | Tampa (Fla.)—History
Classification: LCC NA6846.U62 T36 2026
LC record available at https://lccn.loc.gov/2026010572

The University Press of Florida is the scholarly publishing agency for the State University System of Florida, comprising Florida A&M University, Florida Atlantic University, Florida Gulf Coast University, Florida International University, Florida State University, New College of Florida, University of Central Florida, University of Florida, University of North Florida, University of South Florida, and University of West Florida.

University Press of Florida
PO Box 140239
Gainesville, FL 32614
floridapress.org

GPSR EU Authorized Representative: Mare Nostrum Group B.V., Doelen 72, 4831 GR Breda, The Netherlands, gpsr@mare-nostrum.co.uk

Buildings are living things, possessing individual character and expression. Their personality is as varied as that of humans. They utter a voiceless message that is clear to us who would listen and endeavor to understand.

John Eberson

TRUSS & APPLIANCE COMPANY.
FOOT CORRECTION
SURGICAL GARMENTS
FREE EXAMINATION
TRAINED LADY ATTENDANT
ARCH SUPPORTS
Now PLAYING!
42nd STREET
TAMPA
14 GREAT STARS
42ND. STREET
200
CUT-RATE DRUGS
HALE DRUG CO.
J.M. MERRITT, OWNER
CUT-RATE DRUGS
TAMPA TRUSS & APPLIANCE
The STORE of POPULAR PRICES
CANDY KODAKS
The STORE of POPULAR PRICES
LUCKIES 2-23¢
LUCKIES 2-23¢
200 GLORIOUS GIRLS!
42ND STREET
GO
GO
42nd STREET

CONTENTS

TAMPA THEATRE

1

Downtown Tampa, 1940. Part of Davis Islands and Tampa General Hospital are visible at bottom right. Burgert Brothers Photograph Collection, USF Digital Commons.

Spotlights

The newlywed couple arrived at Tampa's Davis Islands for their honeymoon on October 15, 1926. After settling in, Dolores and Lester Shear went out for the evening and noticed spotlights nearby pointed at the heavens. The streaks of light led the couple across the bridge and into the heart of downtown, where they found a crowd of people pressed around a stately, brightly lit building. The theater's sixty-foot-tall blade sign floating above the throng read "TAMPA" in lights.

Husband and wife were not the only ones feeling giddy that night. Many people in the city, especially those crazy about movies and vaudeville, felt like they were getting hitched, too. Tampa Theatre, designed by John Eberson, famed architect for the stars, looked attractive and unassuming from the outside. But this was not just any movie theater. It was a palace for dreaming and a brilliant new centerpiece for downtown Tampa.

Cigar City

In 1880, Tampa was little more than a village. Outbreaks of yellow fever periodically ravaged the settlement, reducing it to fewer than eight hundred residents. Poor and isolated on the Florida frontier, the town had been incorporated and dissolved a few times. Residents lacked the resources and resolve to sustain a major settlement. Tampa's fortunes changed in 1884 when railroad tycoon Henry Plant connected its sheltered port with the outside world. He also resolved to outdo his friendly rival, Henry Flagler, by building opulent hotels in obscure Florida locales. The Tampa Bay Hotel, with its iconic minarets, opened in 1891 across the Hillsborough River from downtown. By that time, cigar magnates from Cuba had relocated their factories and immigrant workforces from Havana and Key West to a new settlement just outside town. Named Ybor City after cigar baron Vicente Martinez Ybor, it was annexed to the newly founded city of Tampa in 1887. The mixture of immigrants and southern Blacks and Whites helped define the city's cultural identity.

As honeymooners on a stroll, Dolores and Lester Shear happened upon Tampa Theatre's opening night in 1926. Courtesy of Jeff Shear.

The quick growth of Ybor City and West Tampa as centers of cigar production enriched the city culturally and economically. The Cigar City specialized in premium hand-rolled cigars made from "clear Havana" tobacco. The culinary trappings of Havana were everywhere, especially during mealtimes, as the city embraced freshly roasted coffee, black bean soup, arroz con pollo, Cuban bread and sandwiches, guava paste, and cream cheese. The immigrant workforce, mostly Cuban and Spanish at the beginning, was soon augmented by Sicilians and Germans. Tampa boomed in the early 1900s, serving as the hub for trade and shipping on Florida's west coast. People for miles in the hinterland depended on goods and services offered there, often traveling for a day or more to trade—or misbehave. Tampa became notorious as a city wide open to vice. Bolita, an illegal gambling game inspired by Cuba's state lottery, became part of Tampa's everyday routine and spread throughout Florida. Over time, the architecture and rhythms of Havana and the Old World melded into a multicultural Latin Quarter reminiscent of New Orleans. In 1895, West Tampa was founded as another cigar-producing immigrant enclave.

From Tampa's earliest days, Franklin Street was the main drag that reflected the city's progress. The Branch Opera House went up near Franklin and Lafayette Street (today Kennedy Boulevard) in 1884. Two years later, the First National Bank of Tampa built the city's first brick building at Franklin and Washington. The Hillsborough County Courthouse went up in 1892; it opened at about the same time as the Tampa Bay Hotel and shared the same Moorish architectural style favored by architect John Wood. The seedy saloons so common before Prohibition gradually retreated from public view, and a new generation of entertainment asserted itself.

Moving Pictures

It is easy to understand but difficult to explain what makes moving images so deeply compelling. Since the science of cinema gave birth to the moving image, it has

Franklin Street, 1898. Tampa saw explosive growth in a series of booms, fueled mostly by the cigar industry, which depended on foreign-born labor. Burgert Brothers Photograph Collection, USF Digital Commons.

above Movie theaters became a national obsession by the 1920s. The Victory Theater, later renamed the Palace, opened at the corner of Tampa and Zack in 1920 and could accommodate nearly 1,600 guests. Courtesy of Tampa-Hillsborough County Public Library System.

right The Alcazar Theater opened on Franklin Street in 1911. Courtesy of Tampa-Hillsborough County Public Library System.

been irresistible. Moving pictures conquered the world's imagination in less than a generation.

While Tampa first stirred as a city, a new world of art and entertainment was being born based on moving pictures. A variety of contraptions from innovators such as Thomas Edison and the Lumiere brothers amused the public in the 1890s. Edison's kinetoscope helped popularize peep-show parlors and nickelodeons. He also made waves when he released "The Kiss" in 1896. The eighteen-second clip featured more silent talking and nuzzling than kissing, but it enraged America's puritans and delighted most of the rest. The power of cinema was unmistakable, and its potential seemed limitless as a medium of expression. Vaudeville shows incorporated movie shorts as novelty acts in theaters and traveling revues.

Nickelodeons and movie theaters opened in some of Florida's larger towns as the novelty caught on. In 1897, the Park Opera House in Jacksonville was the first in Florida to be converted to show motion pictures. In 1903, before any regular showing of moving pictures in Tampa, a *Tribune* editor joked, "In Tampa they sell bioscope (double-vision) booze—three drinks and then you see the moving pictures." That same year, a minstrel show at the Tampa Bay Hotel's performance space known as the "casino" featured short flicks as an opening act.

Traveling projectionists often showed the first moving pictures in any given community. In 1897, American Biograph may have been the first company to bring moving pictures to the area. Before the construction of Tampa's first nickelodeon, residents gathered at Ball's Grocery on the corner of Franklin and Madison Streets to watch movies projected onto an exterior wall of the building. In her 1966 memoir, resident Susie Kelly Dean recalled the popularity of open-air movies: "The audience would fill the benches on the courthouse square, then overflowed to the steps and curbs nearby. Sometimes vocalists would sing with the picture. The music of the band helped to attract the crowds and made these movie nights seem much more like gala occasions." When traveling acts like Professor Carlisle's Great Wild West Show came to town, they often brought penny arcades with "moving picture machines," traveling nickelodeons.

In 1904, moving pictures were a regular outdoor attraction in Tampa, especially downtown and in Ybor City. Weekly movie shows, projected onto Ybor City's most prominent buildings, aroused the suspicion of the *Tampa Tribune*'s editorial staff. For the sake of the children in attendance, the *Tribune* editorial urged police to regulate the content of screenings, contending that they "bordered very closely on

the vulgar and obscene. If the management must pander to depraved appetites let them rent a hall and present this class of pictures to such as desire to see them. In the minds of the innocent children who flocked to these shows in large numbers, the evil is already done." In 1908, there were "five moving picture shows in Ybor City operating full blast, as the comparatively new innovation has proven popular with the Latin people." Variety acts performed between screenings.

Some of Florida's first dedicated cinemas included the Duval in Jacksonville (opened in 1904), the Palm in St. Petersburg (1905), and Kelly's in Miami (1906). J. L. Ratliff ran one of Tampa's first full-time movie theaters at 315 Franklin Street dating back to 1907. In 1910, there were at least two theaters dedicated to movies: The Favorite downtown (904 Franklin Street) and The Italian in Ybor City. In 1915, there were fourteen movie theaters, six of them on Franklin Street.

above In theaters of the 1920s, live Vaudeville entertainment was a common part of the show. Here, dancers grace the stage of the Casino Theater. Courtesy of Tampa-Hillsborough County Public Library System.

opposite The interior of the Ritz Theater in Ybor City in 1932. The scenery was built into the walls and the sky was painted. Courtesy of Tampa-Hillsborough County Public Library System.

TAMPA BAY HOTEL
SOUTH FLORIDA WHOLESALE GROCERY
BERGER & RACHELSON
WILLIAM TELL FLOUR
MILK
TAMPA ROSSER & FITCH
MERCHANDISE BROKERS
JACKSONVILLE
SWIFT & COMPANY
ARMOUR AND COMPANY
WHOLESALE GROCERS.
CO. WHOLESALE GROCERS.
The old Reliable
HILLSBOROUGH
PURINA

In 1910, one in five Americans patronized nickelodeons every week, but audiences increasingly favored movie theaters. The upper classes tended to view movies with disdain as a vulgar medium for the lower classes. That gradually changed as vaudeville theaters incorporated movies into their variety shows. Feature-length films in the 1910s announced cinema's arrival as an art form worthy of respect. Before long, movies took center stage in vaudeville and eventually supplanted it altogether.

The Boom

In the mid-1920s, Tampa was a city in mid-boom, almost unrecognizable from the destitute village of 1880. The Port of Tampa was thriving. Cigar City surpassed Havana as the global leader in cigar manufacture. Local phosphate mines led the world in fertilizer production. The city annexed West Tampa, bringing another immigrant enclave into the fold. Combining the boom and annexation, the city's population had recently doubled to 100,000, with another 50,000 scattered around Hillsborough County. Downtown Tampa was in its full glory as the central business district.

Wartime austerity during World War I left many citizens flush with cash and a high demand for property. Florida attracted all kinds of people, from tin-can tourists pitching tents in city parks to high rollers with dreams of real estate empires. Gandy Bridge opened in 1924 as the longest automobile toll bridge in the world at the time. The span bound the economies of Tampa and St. Petersburg, helping to create the Tampa Bay market that defines the region today.

The country had discovered the power of speculation, the gamble that any given asset, whether shares of a stock or a piece of property, would increase in value. The Florida land boom boosted Tampa's fortunes, with real estate and construction reaching a fever pitch. In 1923, investors pumped an unprecedented $2 million in construction into the city, a number that doubled the following year. In 1925, Tampa's boom reached its crescendo at a breathtaking $23 million. In 1926 alone, the city saw the completion of more than two thousand new homes, eighty apartment buildings, and a dozen schools and churches.

Bisected by the Hillsborough River, Tampa's waterfront was largely industrialized. Burgert Brothers Photograph Collection, USF Digital Commons.

top As the Florida land boom reached its crescendo in 1925, new construction in the city broke all previous records. Francis Wagner Collection, USF Digital Commons.

bottom Streetcars and Model T Fords vied for space on Franklin Street in 1925. A poster for the Rialto Theater is visible on the streetcar in the foreground. Burgert Brothers Photograph Collection, USF Digital Commons.

In newspaper ads, Tampa's Board of Trade called it "Florida's year-round City" and the Florida Gulf coast's "famous resort Mecca."

> Just outside Tampa over miles of perfect highways, you'll find a paradise of scenic beauty, orange, grapefruit, banana groves; more famous resort places than any other section of Florida can boast of, ever sunny skies, tempered by Gulf breezes, Tampa offers a zestful climate straight through the calendar. In Tampa you'll find the same cosmopolitan atmosphere, the metropolitan shops, hotels, schools, and conveniences of any big northern city. Tampa's famous Latin Quarter will fascinate you with its Spanish restaurants, foreign language music halls, shops and clubs. Don't leave Florida without visiting Tampa [and] opening the door to your greatest opportunity.

Palaces

For millions, movie theaters had become staples of entertainment and an important source of news. Customers visited regardless of what was playing. Theater owners and movie studio moguls built spectacular palaces to draw customers.

Designed by Thomas Lamb and opened in 1913, the Regent Theatre in New York City was the first deluxe movie palace, offering an organ and orchestra to accompany films. The new palatial theater did not catch on with the public until a new manager took over operations. Samuel "Roxy" Rothafel was already a legend in the theater business by the time he was hired to promote the Regent. His ideas revolutionized the industry just as movies were catching on and outgrowing vaudeville. Rothafel "classed up" every aspect of the experience, adopting sharply dressed, well-mannered ushers to whisk patrons to their seats and manage crowds. Lush draperies and carpets signified wealth, and colorful lighting pleased the eye.

Rothafel and his ideas were so successful that he was hired to manage the finest theaters as they opened. Thanks to his savvy leadership, during the 1910s, names such as the Strand Theater, the Rialto, Rivoli, and Capitol—all in New York City—became new standards for the industry. Rothafel's innovations attracted upper- and middle-class patrons to what had previously been a blue-collar experience. The newfound wealth of the studio system was embodied in the larger, more ornate, and well-staffed movie palaces. Like palaces and mansions in real life, movie palaces bestowed status on their occupants, creating the image of extravagance, sophistication, and exclusivity. Their architecture was a marvelous collision of classical sensibilities and those of a more modern age. They functioned as quasi-sacred spaces where people tended to talk in hushed tones.

For a few more cents than at typical theaters, patrons could buy tickets to an exclusive experience at a movie palace. Renowned theater decorator Harold W. Rambusch explained in 1927, "The vast majority of those attending our theaters are of very limited means. Their homes are not luxurious and the theater affords them an opportunity to imagine themselves as wealthy people in luxurious surroundings." At the time, 60 percent of American families lived in poverty. Often dressed in their best clothes, patrons could enact their own scenes and dramas in everyday life that might measure up to the outsized stories they saw on the silver screen.

Architects designed palaces to efficiently manage crowds. At any given time, dozens or even hundreds of people could be waiting for seats in the lobbies of a palace. For their teams of uniformed ushers, handsome, able-bodied young men were favored for crowd control and customer service. The goal of the ushers was to keep the seats filled. As patrons departed, ushers guided new customers to open seats with their flashlights.

Movie palaces showcased cutting-edge technology and the latest architectural innovations. Along with Thomas Lamb and Rapp and Rapp, John Eberson became one of the architects most closely associated with movie palaces. Eberson observed,

> The theater architect must have the ability to present a feasible plan, showing maximum capacity, dependable sight lines and acoustics, proper facilities for quickly seating and dismissing audiences. He must be thoroughly familiar with the engineering problems of a dependable atmospheric conditioning apparatus, which must provide the proper air conditioning of an auditorium. All this with a thorough knowledge of the building market so as to achieve these accomplishments well within the financial appropriation of the theater owner.

In addition to the issues Eberson listed, theater architects also coped with fire protection, lighting, projection, acoustics, ventilation, stage operation, decor, and bulky organ pipes.

In 1925, movie palaces attracted three-quarters of the nation's spending on cinema. Half of the moviegoing public in the nation had ready access to a movie palace by 1930. For every palace, seven smaller theaters competed for customers. Because palaces were usually built in densely populated urban centers, many had retail storefronts and multistory office buildings attached. Major cities across the United States had one or more movie palaces, and smaller towns like Tampa (100,000 residents) and Miami (71,000) were getting the deluxe treatment. Much like the rife speculation in the stock market at the time, the business model of the motion picture industry worked great as long everyone kept buying tickets.

Opera House John

John Eberson was a showman at heart. In 1875, the self-made architect was born in Cernauti, then part of Austria-Hungary, today known as Chernivtsi, Ukraine. His father's success as a timber merchant allowed him to send John to be educated in Dresden and Vienna as an electrical engineer. The young man emigrated to St. Louis in 1901, where he went into business as an electric contractor. He married Beatrice Lamb in 1903, and they started a family.

Eberson's visit to the 1904 World's Fair Louisiana Purchase Exposition turned out to be a date with destiny. There, he was introduced to the magic of motion pictures. He also met Karl Hoblitzelle, another up-and-comer who worked at the expo. Hoblitzelle had just begun investing in vaudeville venues and soon formed the Interstate Theaters Company.

Theater construction was big business at the time, when vaudeville was the dominant form of popular entertainment. Venues all over the country were installing or expanding their electrical systems. All of the lights on the stage and marquee required electrical engineers, so Eberson began much of his working life in theaters. Before leaving St. Louis for Ohio in about 1905, he founded an upstart architectural firm of his own.

John Eberson blossomed from an electrical engineer into a self-taught architect. *Chicago Daily Journal.*

While installing the electrical parts for a theater in Vicksburg, Mississippi, at about the same time, he met George R. Johnson, who ran Johnson Realty and Construction Company, a firm specializing in theater architecture, promotion, and scenic design. They collaborated frequently, and Eberson became steeped in the world of entertainment. Johnson's firm spent most of its time in smaller towns building theaters using standard designs. Working with him closely, Eberson picked

Built in 1915, the Paramount in Austin still stands today. Eberson's earlier work earned him the nickname "Opera House John," but his artistic ambitions found their best home in movie palaces. Courtesy of Mike Hume.

up on the intricacies of theater construction and worked in a variety of roles, from engineer to scene painter. Through this rigorous introduction, he learned all the facets of designing theaters; eventually he led Johnson's architecture department and earned the nickname "Opera House John."

In 1910, success and ambition drew Eberson to Chicago, which was a hotbed of elaborate theater design at the time. He worked closely with Karl Hoblitzelle and his influential Interstate Theaters Company. Eberson reminisced to *Motion Picture News* in 1926,

> I have served a long apprenticeship in theater design, during which time I have met men and conditions of all kinds, and to have played a part in the development of the amusement business, with its kaleidoscopic changes, has been an education in itself. It has been most interesting to see the development of potent chains of theaters under the guidance of my old friends and clients.

Between 1914 and 1922, four thousand new theaters opened in the United States, and Eberson built his share of them. His firm had become one of the top three theater design companies in the United States.

Inspiration

No one who met John Eberson forgot him. He was friendly and talkative with a goofy sense of humor and a dramatic sense of style. Elsa Eberson Kyle described her father as a larger-than-life character.

> He had a great flair for the dramatic, in his dress and in his surroundings. Never did things in an ordinary way. If he liked something he didn't buy one, he bought five or six. All special designs, car bodies, interiors, radiator hood emblems, colors, etc. Not one chow dog but a kennel of chow dogs, it was the same with horses. His clothes are all custom made and designed by him, black velvet vests with many jet buttons and a white pique edging along the lapels,

Like his theaters, Eberson himself had a big personality and grand sense of style. Courtesy of Maury and Nancy Brassert.

> a brown cape with a velvet collar, black homburg hat, and flowing black artist tie. He had a strong, forceful character, and when he entered a room his presence was felt. Dynamic might be the word, a true showman.

John Eberson grew tired of the staid designs of most movie houses. "Today's average theater is virtually a replica of yesterday's, except that it is more elaborately dressed up," he explained. Opera houses and early movie palaces at the time adhered to Victorian clichés intended to impress the rich, such as marble, gold leaf, massive chandeliers, and box seating in balconies for elite patrons. The end result was grand but cold and uninviting. Their exclusive nature seemed to contradict the collective experience of cinema, lacking whimsy and charm.

"To impress the public with mass and grandeur of proportion is the art and skill of the office building and railway depot designer," Eberson quipped. The architect sensed that the new age of movie palaces called for something different than another overserious opera house. As his competitors began to experiment with more innovative designs, so did he. His new concepts would be dreamy and daring, an "architecture of fancy." Eberson explained, "We are fully convinced that what the public wants is something 'different,' artistic and colorful, it must have texture and punch. We must please the broad masses, and in most cases they do not know art, but rather feel it."

Eberson took inspiration from Daniel Burnham, the chief architect of the 1893 World's Columbian Exposition in Chicago. Burnham had used "staff," plaster reinforced with straw, to cheaply construct a massive neoclassical White City on the drained swamps of Chicago. When illuminated with dramatic electric lighting, the massive halls and temples dazzled millions of visitors as visions of beauty and order. It seemed Burham had conjured a model city replete with gardens, statues, fountains, and canals out of practically nothing.

The influence of the White City was evident in the design of the St. Louis World's Fair in 1904. Upon Eberson's visit to that fair, the elaborate, soaring buildings impressed him. He was especially intrigued by the fair's use of plaster staff to create such impressive sets and structures. When molded and dried, it could be painted to look like stone, tile, statues, virtually anything. The fair and its buildings in Chicago and St. Louis came and went like dreams, since the elaborate campuses were merely stage sets to be torn down at the end of the performance.

The world's fairs were designed to evoke visions of timeless grandeur. Eberson

Eberson's visit to the St. Louis World's Fair in 1904 was life-changing for the spectacles he saw and the people he met. Library of Congress.

wanted to emulate that. While the designs of the world's fairs mimicked ancient Greece and Rome, Eberson was deeply influenced by the Romantic architecture of Vienna, where he lived as a young man. For instance, St. Stephen's Cathedral is a gothic, Romanesque wonder completed in 1578 that still stands today. The Vienna State Opera House (1869) and the Burgtheater (1888) are also good examples of spaces that may have influenced Eberson's vision.

The architect's style evolved, and he edged toward something unique: grand, dreamy, and a little mysterious. Eberson found that the Sunshine State supplied some inspiration of its own:

> I have been wintering in Florida for the past several years, and it is from the state that I got the atmospheric idea. I was impressed with the colorful scenes which greeted me at Miami, Palm Beach, and Tampa. Visions of Italian gardens, Spanish patios, Persian shrines and French formal gardens flashed

Eberson was intrigued by the use of plaster bound with horse hair, called "staff," to create decor and sculptures that appear to be stone. Here, a worn piece of plaster reveals the hair beneath. Courtesy of Jeff Fay.

> through my mind, and at once I directed my energies to carrying out these ideas. I saw the value of putting nature to work and so have borrowed the color tones and designs that are found in the flowers and trees. The inhabitants of Spain and southern Italy live under the sun and enjoy the happiness nature affords them. So I decided their architecture probably would provide the best foundation for a theater. Correct use of lights, artificial foliage, beautiful furniture, statuary, mirrors, pottery pieces and plumed birds produce the effect.

Atmospheric Theaters

Early in his career, Eberson was not positioned to win contracts to build the finest movie palaces. Much of his work came from outside the biggest movie markets. Established firms such as Thomas Lamb and Rapp and Rapp dominated the best clients, but that began to change in the 1920s. Eberson's increasingly unique movie palaces proved that he had outgrown the "Opera House John" nickname and was among the best in the world.

Eberson is best known for merging architecture and theater set design in his signature "atmospheric" style. This new breed of theaters featured auditoriums designed like massive outdoor stage sets. The open-air illusion was maintained by a ceiling that appeared to be a starlit dark-blue sky with projected clouds drifting over the audience. Every atmospheric theater featured a different scene that conjured a timeless (usually Mediterranean) setting under the stars. Some even featured sunrise, sunset, and moonrise lighting sequences. Making his grand outdoor illusions look convincing required the use of perspective and asymmetry often employed in set design.

The atmospheric concept energized venues with an illusion, incorporating the audience and the entertainment into a fantasy. Eberson's atmospherics "produced an almost religious experience," curator Jane Preddy wrote in a 1990 exhibition catalog, "a breathlessness when the lights lowered and the stars began to sparkle through lazily moving white clouds. It was escapist and somehow effortless."

Eberson's evolution toward the atmospheric style was already evident as he constructed the Dallas Majestic (1921), and the Houston Majestic (1923) is considered to be his first true atmospheric movie palace.

Eberson remarked on his new style,

Defies Ancient Theatre Building Tradition

Panorama of auditorium of the Majestic, Houston, Tex., designed by John Eberson. On the left the proscenium represents an Italian palace and pergola. On the right is represented a terraced garden and temple. Graduated colored lighting effects, casting light from coves up to ceiling and properly placed automatic cloud machines together with electrical twinkling stars create a perfect illusion of a Mediterranean sky going from bright daylight to a soft moonlight.

Proscenium on right showing terraced garden and temple

Proscenium on left showing Italian palace and pergola

Eberson's Houston Majestic (1923) is considered his first fully "atmospheric" theater, depicting an outdoor scene under a starry sky. *Motion Picture News.*

> We visualize and dream a magnificent amphitheater up under a glorious moonlit sky in an Italian garden, in a Persian court, in a Spanish patio, or in a mystic Egyptian temple-yard, all canopied by soft moonlit sky. [Atmospherics] convert the theater auditorium into a meeting place surrounded by nature's setting. Few innovations in the theater business have taken root as quickly as the atmospheric theater. To make the illusion perfect requires not only a thorough understanding and knowledge of Old World architecture, but we must also know how to transform and create these antique soft textures and the interestingly polychromed buildings with modern tools and artcraft.

Eberson's use of color was sophisticated and subtle. He believed that red was an unlucky hue for theaters, so he used it sparingly, favoring earthier tones. The simulated canopy of the night sky was his signature touch, bathing his prosceniums with a seductive dark blue. Eberson explained the importance of calibrating the color to produce the desired effect:

> An atmospheric theater based on nature's school of color harmony is art which is felt by everybody. This new form of theater caters to those who do not possess educated tastes. Color is the most important instrument to create effects and influence the appreciative mind and sensitive soul of the public. We credit the deep azure blue of the Mediterranean sky with a therapeutic value, soothing the nerves and calming perturbing thoughts. It is in the softly lighted foyers and in the blue-domed auditoriums that our mesmerism is performed. It releases the nerve tension of the audience, refreshes the eye, makes one feel that one can breathe. Blue is always described as the color of hope. This is not a fanciful and trivial sentiment, but a fact which can be scientifically proved, but it must be a certain, defined and distinct blue on a certain defined and distinct textured surface. We strive to use more art and less tedious methods of decorating to get our effects.

Eberson occasionally told stories that provided some insight into his creative process. His chief designer and aide, A. C. Liska, was an important collaborator going back to 1909. Together, they found whimsical inspiration even in trivial objects, Eberson said. While rummaging antique shops in New Orleans, they found "an ancient pierced brass jewel-studded Persian incense burner" that inspired the Avalon Theater they built in Chicago (1927).

> Then and there was born the idea and scheme for a Persian theater. Persia, the land of the turquoise and the rose, the land of the sacred shrine, blue and gold. The richly grilled and torridly embellished palace on the left, the tall walls of a Persian rose garden on the right, the sacred pilgrim's fountain and shrine in the left side niche, the heavily barred and shuttered entrance to the sacred city courtyard on the right side of the main stage. Mystic pierced brass lanterns, rich tent hangings, colorful mosaic panels, richly carved and polychromed wooden ceiling beams, intricate marble Moorish pattern floors, jeweled door heads, mirrored curtains, fragrant bowers of roses, all under the starlit sky of the near east, a softly mysterious but interesting scheme for a modern theater auditorium.

Although no one would accuse Eberson's atmospherics of being restrained, his designs were judicious and full of subtleties. "We believe in ornament," Eberson admitted, "and are prepared to be lavish with it, but we are diligently cautious not to infringe upon the canons of good taste by avoiding over-design and over-elaborateness, which only achieve vulgarity." In his 1928 book *The American Architecture of Today,* G. H. Edgell commented on Eberson's atmospherics, "One might expect that the building would be vulgar. Actually it is a fairyland, inviting and compelling the visitor to accept its imaginative and exotic point of view."

Much of the design would be dimly illuminated, especially during shows. Therefore, Eberson insisted that decor had to be "seen in the dark and felt in the dark. Color and the combination of color; the play of light and shadows; textures; shapes and silhouettes must be blended into a plan."

Writing for *National Magazine,* Frances Mather described Eberson as "a man of great conceptions, carried out to the tiniest practical detail. Employing many arts, Mr. Eberson is at once architect, engineer, interior decorator and mural painter, using the artificial lighting as well as brushes to gain his color effect and he applies all this knowledge in creating his contribution to the modern theater—The outdoor illusion."

Atmospherics had a magical effect on the audience, Jane Preddy observed,

> Eberson's stroke of genius lay in extending the theatrical illusions previously confined to the stage into the space of the auditorium. The magic of the movie experience was made much more compelling by implicating the reality of the audience space in the illusion. With only a little effort of the imagination, the

Eberson built the Majestic Theatre in San Antonio (*right*) and the Paramount in Anderson, Indiana, in 1929 as his atmospheric style peaked in popularity. Courtesy of Mike Hume.

audience would believe that they were settled in a Mediterranean courtyard watching the sun gradually set and the stars slowly appear among the puffy clouds scudding across the sky. The movies had found the perfect architectural foil for their innate capacity to create illusion.

The moviegoing public enthusiastically agreed. Between 1923, when the Houston Majestic opened, and 1930, Eberson built more than 160 theaters around the world, including about thirty atmospherics around the United States. Theater architects across the country faithfully copied his designs. Eberson completed his last atmospheric, Loew's Paradise in the Bronx, in 1929. Along with the Paradise, Tampa Theatre is one of eighteen Eberson atmospherics still standing today.

Practical Plans

While elevating the theatrical experience, Eberson's designs employed techniques that saved his clients money. He was fond of sharing his "creed for theater architects," something he called the "nine little Ps. Prepare Practical Plans for Pretty Playhouses—Please Patrons—Pay Profits." He took the part about "practical plans" seriously.

Although his finished interior designs looked dreamy, Eberson (*far right*) emphasized "practical plans." Courtesy of Maury and Nancy Brassert.

Atmospheric theaters cost a quarter less than the hard-top designs of his competitors. Replacing the weighty opera-house chandeliers with the starry sky saved costs on the heavy beams and rafters that would have been necessary to suspend them above the audience. Eberson eschewed the typical imported marble, cut-glass chandeliers, and French damask for much cheaper, lighter building materials that looked equally impressive. Using plaster staff in place of marble and stone saved money and reduced the weight his theaters had to bear.

One common challenge when building palaces in far-flung locations was the lack of skilled labor to produce the intricate interiors they required. Eberson and his wife, Beatrice, founded Michel Angelo Studios, a plaster casting com-

Michel Angelo Studios promoted its sophisticated use of color and highlighted Tampa Theatre as an example in this 1926 ad. *Motion Picture News,* Internet Archive.

pany that molded standardized fixtures in Chicago and shipped them to worksites. There, employees unpacked and installed the decor for his theaters. Michel Angelo Studios' highly trained team allowed Eberson more control over the process and final product.

Eberson's son, Drew, joined the firm in 1926 and later recalled the role of Michel Angelo Studios and the roving installation team:

> Sometimes area architects were hired to get us by the local inspectors, but most of the time Father controlled the entire operation through our own supervisor. They moved from theater to theater installing the plaster ornamentation, the statuary, trees and birds, painting the walls. They hung the banners my mother and sisters made. My job was ordering and placing the statuary, mapping out the stars, and generally seeing to it that things went well. The ornamentation for the walls and ceiling was cast plaster and produced from clay molds. As for the lighting fixtures, we designed them ourselves, then had them made in Chicago by Pearlman. Father used a lot of pink lightbulbs, and since they were impossible to buy, he dipped them in pink paint. The tapestries? Many of them were from a theater supply company in New York, the furniture also, and from antique shops in New Orleans.

At home and in his theaters, Eberson favored medieval-looking artifacts such as suits of armor, swords, heraldic banners, and crests as ornaments. His signature stuffed peacock always appeared with its tail feathers down, perhaps the only sign of modesty in his buildings.

The sculptures in Eberson's theaters looked like they could have been shipped directly from the Louvre. The P. P. Caproni and Brother firm in Boston created exact plaster replicas of works from Paris and Athens molded from old statues. After having its surface distressed to suggest aging, the finished product was virtually indistinguishable from stone. Adopting an antique look, Eberson was fond of pointing out, reduced the need for maintenance, since it was not meant to look new.

Eberson's home featured the same ornate plasterwork and decor as in his theaters. A family portrait he commissioned also reflects his fantastical sense of style. Courtesy of Maury and Nancy Brassert.

Paramount

Like many other future titans of the motion picture industry, Hungarian immigrant Adolph Zukor recognized the potential of the medium early. He left the fur and design business behind in 1903 and went on to form a chain of penny arcades with hand-cranked viewing devices. As movies became more practical, Zukor and others wanted to make them more acceptable to the middle class, which would require the industry to "kill the slum tradition," as he put it.

Zukor pioneered moviemaking at every level and demonstrated the power of vertical integration and monopoly. He accumulated an impressive stable of talent (including names such as Fairbanks, Pickford, Valentino, and Swanson) and formed Paramount Pictures. To sell its products to the public, Paramount founded Publix Theatres in 1925. During the next four years, the chain became the biggest in the country, with an especially strong presence in Texas and the Southeast, including Florida, with its growing market of 350 theaters.

In 1926, downtown Tampa was Publix territory. The chain already ran the Strand Theater (on Twiggs Street), the Seminole (Florida Avenue), Victory (Tampa Street), and the Franklin and Grand Theaters on Franklin Street, the thoroughfare that best showcased Tampa's economic health. Lined with banks and department stores such as Maas Brothers and Kress, Franklin Street was the place to shop, socialize, and be entertained.

The Maas Brothers department store was one of downtown's commercial keystones. Several of its executives had dreams of building a movie palace nearby. President Jerome Waterman was not a typical executive. A driven daredevil, he had one of the first pilot's licenses in the country. He was even said to have flown with the Wright brothers. The high-flying entrepreneur must have known that Publix Theatres was a natural partner—and perhaps his only option—to realize a dream palace in Tampa.

As president of Consolidated Amusements Corporation as well as Maas Brothers, Waterman was joined by fellow executive Charles McKay, doctor Lewis A. Bize, and attorney Hilton Hampton, but there was a catch. The main investors did not own the prime real estate they wanted on Franklin Street. But one of the investor's brothers did. Gainesville attorney William Wade Hampton refused to sell the property, which he had purchased in 1899, but agreed to a long-term lease. In retrospect, the plan seemed like building a heavy castle on soft sand.

Publix Theatres delivered a promise of quality ahead of opening their newest location. *Tampa Tribune,* 1926.

John Eberson's design for Tampa Theatre's auditorium. John and Drew Eberson Papers, Wolfsonian, Florida International University.

At age eleven, Charles Bardin served as an office boy for several big firms with headquarters downtown. Jerome Waterman called on him to make various deliveries. Bardin recalled,

The Maas Brothers company grew from a humble haberdashery into Tampa's signature department store. Hampton Dunn Postcard Collection, USF Digital Commons.

> He did this quite often. He'd give me a bag of money and the receipts from Maas to deposit over here at the corner, the National City Bank. From his fourth-floor office, he could look down and see me across the street. He could watch me go into the bank. I was a kid, and I would take this paper bag of money and deposit it, of course it could be checks and cash, and he'd always tell me, "Charlie, don't you talk to anybody and don't you ever tell anybody that you carry these bags of money to the bank." Everybody thought I had my lunch. One day, he called me into his office. He gave me an envelope this time and said, "Charlie, in this envelope is a check for $150,000 to start the building of the Tampa Theatre."

And so it began.

Construction

At roughly one-third of an acre, the available property on Franklin Street was too small for the sprawling palaces found in New York and Chicago. Tampa Theatre would be far more intimate than those cavernous palaces, with roughly 1,400 seats split between the floor and mezzanine. Eberson preferred smaller theaters and refused to compromise audience satisfaction with oversized auditoriums, capping his own projects at 4,200 seats.

Contractor G. A. Miller broke ground in April 1925, and his crew went to the task of building the structure, which included a ten-story office tower above the lobby.

Beginning in 1924, billboards heralded the coming of Tampa's very own movie palace. Courtesy of Tampa-Hillsborough County Public Library System.

Miller was one of the leading contractors in the state, having also built towers such as the Floridan Hotel and Peninsular Telephone Company office building.

In 1926, an estimated fifteen thousand people attended the city's theaters every evening. Many of them passed by the construction site on Franklin Street looking forward to the day they could set foot in their own movie palace. Young Frances Fontaine was especially excited. Her father worked on the construction site and told her about what he saw. "He used to come home and tell us how beautiful it was inside. He told us that there were stars twinkling in the sky and that we would be able to see them when we watched a movie."

Tickets for the opening gala went on sale at M. L. Price's music store (Tampa and Zack Streets) two days before the event. At seventy-five cents each, eager residents snapped up the 1,600 tickets in just two hours.

Publix Theatres placed large ads in the newspapers heralding a new age.

> Tonight a procession of the pleasure loving people of Tampa will lead to the new Tampa theater. They will come away with the news that Tampa has one of the most beautiful theaters in the world! Positively luxurious! Perfectly serviced! And a marvelous show! Its beauty will leave you breathless and the entertainment will hold you spellbound. We who have Publix theaters in fifty cities from New York to San Francisco are proud of the new Tampa as we are of no other theater in the chain. It is the last word in luxury and splendor—a

Another Eberson atmospheric, Miami's Olympia Theatre, opened in February 1926 and still stands today. Florida Memory.

Like many movie palaces, the Tampa Theatre building included an office tower to maximize floor space. John and Drew Eberson Papers, Wolfsonian, Florida International University.

Tampa Theatre opened just as the Florida land boom went bust. John and Drew Eberson Papers, Wolfsonian, Florida International University.

The building included small retail spaces behind the auditorium on Florida Avenue that have since been absorbed into the theater's operational footprint. John and Drew Eberson Papers, Wolfsonian, Florida International University.

Section C TAMPA MORNING TRIBUNE Section C

Magnificent New Tampa Theater Opens To Night

On Tampa Theatre's opening day, the *Tampa Morning Tribune* featured portraits of VIPs from Publix Theatres and Consolidated Amusements. 1926. *Tampa Tribune.*

magnificent jewel of great beauty that we have set in Tampa for your pleasure and pride. Tonight we turn it over to you. Tonight's the night!

Opening

On opening night, the large illuminated blade sign and brilliant marquee above Franklin Street lit the way for an eager crowd. Knowing that "the show begins on the sidewalk," Eberson wanted to attract plenty of attention with his signs. "I try to capitalize every watt of light efficiently," he explained, to utilize the full brilliance of an exposed-bulb lamp where needed.

"I try to create an unusual 'bright spot,'" he revealed, "covering the building as well as the sidewalks."

The evening's printed program featured an exhibit catalog for the many sculptures around the theater. A journalist noted, "The theater began to fill long before the program started, and the lobby, foyers, mezzanines and parlors, with their antiques and colorful decorations were the centers of much admiration. Expressions of praise

From the opening program, 1926. Tampa Theatre.

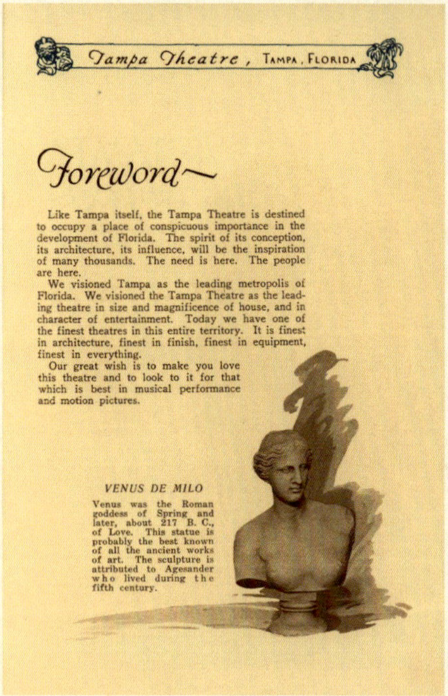

Tampa Theatre, Tampa, Florida

Foreword~

Like Tampa itself, the Tampa Theatre is destined to occupy a place of conspicuous importance in the development of Florida. The spirit of its conception, its architecture, its influence, will be the inspiration of many thousands. The need is here. The people are here.

We visioned Tampa as the leading metropolis of Florida. We visioned the Tampa Theatre as the leading theatre in size and magnificence of house, and in character of entertainment. Today we have one of the finest theatres in this entire territory. It is finest in architecture, finest in finish, finest in equipment, finest in everything.

Our great wish is to make you love this theatre and to look to it for that which is best in musical performance and motion pictures.

VENUS DE MILO

Venus was the Roman goddess of Spring and later, about 217 B. C., of Love. This statue is probably the best known of all the ancient works of art. The sculpture is attributed to Agesander who lived during the fifth century.

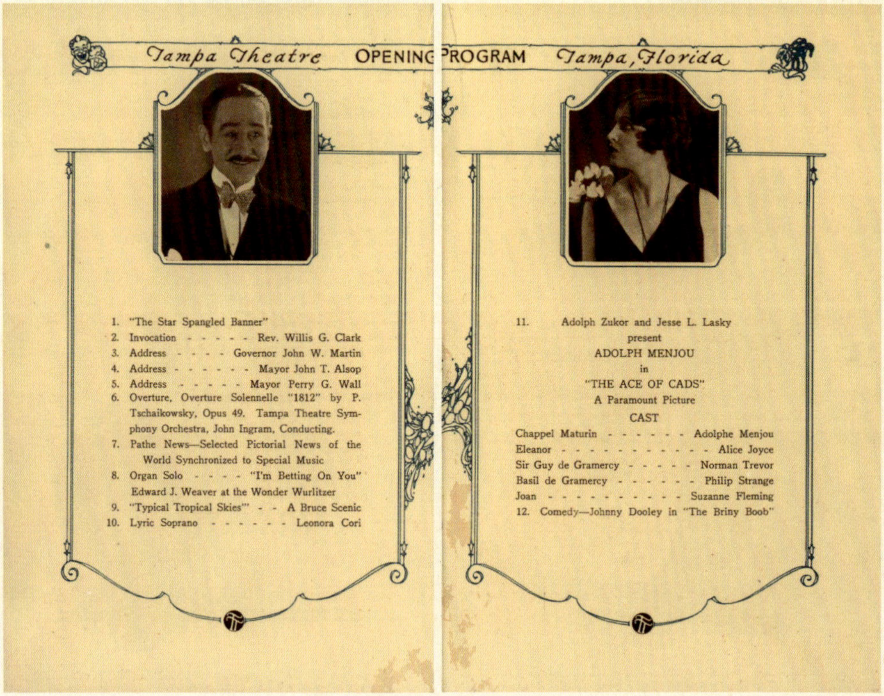

Tampa Theatre OPENING PROGRAM Tampa, Florida

1. "The Star Spangled Banner"
2. Invocation - - - - - - Rev. Willis G. Clark
3. Address - - - - Governor John W. Martin
4. Address - - - - - - - Mayor John T. Alsop
5. Address - - - - - - Mayor Perry G. Wall
6. Overture, Overture Solennelle "1812" by P. Tschaikowsky, Opus 49. Tampa Theatre Symphony Orchestra, John Ingram, Conducting.
7. Pathe News—Selected Pictorial News of the World Synchronized to Special Music
8. Organ Solo - - - - "I'm Betting On You" Edward J. Weaver at the Wonder Wurlitzer
9. "Typical Tropical Skies" - - A Bruce Scenic
10. Lyric Soprano - - - - - - - Leonora Cori
11. Adolph Zukor and Jesse L. Lasky present ADOLPH MENJOU in "THE ACE OF CADS" A Paramount Picture

CAST

Chappel Maturin - - - - - - - Adolphe Menjou
Eleanor - - - - - - - - - - - - - Alice Joyce
Sir Guy de Gramercy - - - - - Norman Trevor
Basil de Gramercy - - - - - - Philip Strange
Joan - - - - - - - - - - - - - Suzanne Fleming

12. Comedy—Johnny Dooley in "The Briny Boob"

were heard on all sides as Tampans viewed for the first time the new million-dollar theater which the Consolidated Amusements, Inc., has built for the city."

Opening night's program began with an invocation by Reverend Willis G. Clark, rector of St. Andrew's Episcopal Church. Judge Raleigh Petteway, a popular speaker about town, was master of ceremonies. Director of public relations for Publix Theatres (and mayor of Jacksonville) John T. Alsop introduced the leadership of Consolidated Amusements. Hometown Mayor Perry G. Wall spoke about the educational value of movies and accepted the theater as if it was a gift to the people of Tampa. John Ingram's twenty-piece orchestra played Tchaikovsky's "1812 Overture." A scenic film was followed by a novelty sing-along, "I'm Betting on You," played by organist Eddie Weaver on the Mighty Wurlitzer Theater Organ. Soprano Leonora Cori enchanted the audience with her renditions of "Care Nome" and a ballad

Two years after opening, the theater disbanded its impressive orchestra, a casualty of "talkies" and more sophisticated audio speakers. The orchestra pit visible in this photo would eventually be covered with an extended stage. Florida Memory.

After performing with the San Carlo Opera Company in the mid-1920s, lyric soprano Leonora Cori began touring in revues and as a solo act and appeared at Tampa Theatre throughout its opening week. She continued on the Publix and Fox theater circuits and performed regularly on radio throughout the 1930s. Music Division, New York Public Library for the Performing Arts.

In the 1920s, what was then known as Carrier Engineering Corporation provided climate control systems to theaters around the country. *Motion Picture News*, 1926. Internet Archive.

and received a "storm of applause." The program culminated in *The Ace of Cads,* a feature film with leads Adolphe Menjou and Alice Joyce. A brief two-reel comedy concluded the evening's program.

Of all the technological innovations embedded in Tampa Theatre, perhaps none was more universally welcome than the "cool, fresh, crisp air driven through the entire house" by a climate-control system. The Carrier Engineering Corporation supplied the state-of-the-art air conditioner at a cost of $78,000. Publix Theatres mandated a constant temperature of 72 degrees and a relative humidity of 55 percent. Even if the house was packed with customers, Publix only tolerated a deviation by one degree. At last there was a refuge from Florida's steamy summer months. The temperature control also attracted couples who could finally dress to the nines

As the first commercially air-conditioned building in the city, the theater's "man-made air" heralded in headlines at the time suffused the space with luxury. Hampton Dunn Postcard Collection, USF Digital Commons.

Textured walls and tapestries contributed to the interior's timeless feel. John and Drew Eberson Papers, Wolfsonian, Florida International University.

without breaking a sweat. Still, some were wary of the newfangled system and the air that it blew. Publix Theatres assured the public, "No drafts are produced and there's no possibility of one becoming ill from the air as it is much more pure than that breathed on the street." The theater's best advertisement may have been the nearby streetcar stop, where commuters might feel the cool air wafting out the front door as they walked by.

Miracles did not seem out of place in Eberson's latest movie palace. The *Tampa Daily Times* rhapsodized that it was like

> some temple of the past, devoted to the arts, some forgotten place rediscovered and brought from Mediterranean shores. Mellow shaded lights on their tall wrought iron stands, elaborately carved chests and chairs, reminiscent of past Spanish and Italian decades, statuary, rich wall hangings, medieval and early Italian portrait paintings, medallions, coats of arms, all play their part here. One by one these myriad features, employed in recapturing an old mood in this newest playhouse, are fitted into place in an effect indescribably soft and restful.
>
> It was difficult to ascertain which pleased most, the beauty of the theater itself, or the enjoyable dedicatory program. Both combined left an impression which will linger long with those fortunate enough to obtain seats for the first night performance.

Exit Eberson

In Lakeland, Florida, John E. Melton dreamed of building his own atmospheric palace. While the Polk Theater in Lakeland was under construction, its architect, James E. Casale, just so happened to keep his office in the Tampa Theatre building. Perhaps his location made it easier to study and copy Eberson's handiwork up close. When the project ran out of funds, Publix Theatres bought the Polk and completed it in 1928. The end result was a loving imitation of Eberson's atmospheric projects. In 1927, Jacksonville got the 2,200-seat Florida Theater in the heart of the city. It featured romantic atmospheric lobbies and Spanish-tile eaves spilling over with flowering vines. The architects, Robert E. Hall and Roy A. Benjamin, tellingly used fixtures from Michel Angelo Studios to get that authentic Eberson look.

Beatrice (Lamb) Eberson joined her husband, John, as a founder of Michel Angelo Studios and brought her eye for interior design to his projects. Courtesy of Maury and Nancy Brassert.

Drew Eberson joined his father's architecture firm in 1926. Here they appear in their New York office. Courtesy of Maury and Nancy Brassert.

Eberson called the Tampa his favorite atmospheric theater and said, "Tampa has a landmark of which it can be justly proud." His personal mascot was the peacock, and each of his theaters contained a stuffed bird somewhere in the auditorium. As in all of his theaters, upon completion, the architect placed a burlap sack of bird seed on the stage and pinned a note to it that read, "Something for the birds after I'm gone." Eberson never returned to Tampa Theatre.

Movie-palace decorator Harold Rambusch wrote at the time, "The atmospheric has met with reasonable success. It has been done effectively and the public has taken to it, but it is essentially so sophisticated and unnatural that there is grave doubt that it will long survive." The demand for Eberson's atmospherics fell with the stock market crash in 1929. After the debacle, Eberson continued to design theaters but opted for restrained styles such as Art Deco and Streamline Moderne that he confessed he did not enjoy as much as his atmospherics. He continued to design and build until 1951 or so, but the theater business would never be the same. John Eberson designed more than five hundred buildings over fifty years, including one hundred movie palaces. In 1954, Eberson died in New York at age seventy-nine.

"Everyone in downtown knew me." During her forty-six years in the box office, Blondelle Pate Gladney was the smiling face of Tampa Theatre. 1973. © Tampa Bay Times/Zuma Press.

Gladney put her stamp of approval on the new Jerry Lewis film in 1958. *Tampa Tribune*.

2

The Box Office Queen

Tampa Theatre couldn't open soon enough for eighteen-year-old Blondelle Gladney (then Pate). She had watched its construction and wanted a job at the dream palace. "It was beautiful. It was just so exciting," she recalled. When she finally got inside, she was swept away by the theater and the glamor it represented. "It was just like being in heaven," she said wistfully.

She found that the box office cashier position was not for the faint of heart. In addition to the crowds of ticket buyers, her many duties overwhelmed her at first. She managed the cash and filled out financial reports. The box office telephone rang constantly. Reserving seats was another big responsibility, especially when popular movies promised to fill the house. Her workdays were long, from around noon until after midnight. Management did not permit her to take time off. Gladney even visited a doctor for her raw nerves. She soon found her footing and was chosen to train other cashiers around the state, including at the sister Eberson atmospheric, the Olympia Theatre in Miami.

The box office position was demanding but also had its benefits for a social butterfly like Gladney, who looked like a starlet herself. Dressed to the nines with meticulously styled hair and makeup, she became a Tampa Theatre icon, a vision of beauty behind glass who could converse with anyone. "I love to talk," she said years later, "that's why I have so many friends. I talked to everybody that came in, 'Good morning, how are you? Good afternoon, how are you?' I'd start a conversation." An arrangement with a neighboring business benefited them both, she recalled: "Jack, the man at the beauty shop, used to give me my hairdos for nothing, just to advertise his work. I gave him so much business, everybody would come to the box office and say, 'Your hair is just beautiful. Who does it?' I'd say, 'Jack across the street.' I was into everything. Everyone in downtown knew me."

A favorite memory she shared was going out drinking with the ushers on a night out.

> It was against the rules for us to run around with the ushers. The manager said, "I'll fire any one of you if I catch you out with one of the ushers or the assistant managers." We all were out at the Columbia Restaurant one night. I was out there with all these ushers. Me and the candy girl, about twenty of us, had a dining room together. My God who walked in but the district manager and the president of the company. We were scared to death. We all knew we were fired, and so I went up to Mr. Clark, and I said, "Am I going to get fired?" He said, "No honey, they said they'd forgive you this time." I'll never forget that night.

If the district manager himself hadn't been smitten with her, they might have lost their jobs. Her radiant personality shone in the box office long after the theater began to fade. With her glamorous looks and down-to-earth personality, she elevated her role in the box office and made it truly special, staying for forty-six years. There will never be another quite like her.

March of the Ushers

In 1929, Charles Bardin, who years earlier delivered the check that launched its construction, aspired to be an usher at the Tampa Theatre. At age seventeen, he applied for a job and was asked to come in for an interview. The next day, the high school senior rushed to the theater after class. Chief usher Sidney Elliott interviewed him briefly, then led him to the basement to be fitted with a uniform and be inspected by Blondelle. It was common knowledge that she, the box office manager, was the ultimate gatekeeper. She wanted handsome ushers at Tampa Theatre.

Rigorous inspections occurred at the start of every shift, scrutinizing hair, shoes, and attire. The chief usher trained Bardin in the ways of customer relations. "He showed me how to greet and talk to people. I was told exactly what to say and how to say it," Bardin said. A salesman from Swobilt's, a menswear store nearby, paid regular visits to see if the ushers wanted something more comfortable and stylish than the suits that came with the job. Bardin was measured backstage at the theater and recalled, "You could have the pockets any way you wanted them, on a slant. You could have the lapels wide or narrow, and he'd do all that for twenty dollars." Swobilt's allowed ushers to put two dollars down and pay off the rest over several paydays.

Former usher Charles Bardin and his wife, Ellen, sat for an interview in the late 1990s with Janna Jones and Tara Schroeder (*far left*). Tampa Theatre.

An usher's primary function was to keep seats filled as customers came and went with little regard for show times. Back then, movie theaters were like televisions in the nation's living room that ran all day. Tampa Bay History Center.

Like all starting ushers, Bardin began working in the second tier of the balcony. He was promoted to the first tier and worked his way down to the main floor. He became responsible for hiring and training ushers as well as greeting people as they arrived, right after the doorman greeted them. On nights with especially long lines outside, ushers kept the lines orderly as customers waited. Bardin explained,

> There was a lot of pomp and circumstance. This was a real posh place to take your date out on the town. It was very common that we'd have to send some of the ushers outside to keep people in line. That was common every night, to have a crowd on the corner waiting to come in.
>
> The first thing that you came into when you walked in was the doorman in a big heavy coat like you see at the hotels, lots of gold braid on top. He'd take tickets and say good evening. Then just inside, there would be the chief usher and maybe his assistant. I would direct you down the aisle. The ushers had to be on their toes all the time because the theater was pretty dark and you would have to keep your eye out to watch for vacant (or broken) seats. At the time if there were any children crying, we were instructed immediately to go and ask, "Would you like to take the little one to the ladies room?" or something like that. I got hit one time because I told the lady that. At the Strand Theater, I said that one time and the guy hit me and knocked me out.

During shift changes, the relief ushers marched in formation around the theater. Projectionist Joe Paleveda recalled, "It was like a changing of the guard. They'd march up the aisle, drop a guy off, and the guy who just got replaced would get in the back of the line. Then they'd go to the next post and the next guy in line would take his post. It was really official because the Tampa Theatre was a deluxe operation." Manager Jack L. Hobby remembered the high standards of training: "We drilled those boys in courtesy and carriage as if they were at West Point."

Ushers were a handsome welcome but also security who kept order in the theater. Although the young men were often still in high school, they commanded respect and were a reassuring presence for single women and children. Writing in the *New Republic,* Lloyd Lewis reported that by day, movie palaces belonged to women: "In the dim auditoriums which seem to float in a world of dream and where the people brushing on either side are safely remote, an American woman may spend her afternoon alone." Blondelle Gladney said she noticed that trend at Tampa Theatre:

“We had a lot of girls who used to come in by themselves. They’d bring their books after school. At nighttime they usually came with dates.” Betty Phipps recalled when as a girl she attended Saturday matinees there with four or five friends: “With matching silk socks and hair ribbons, color-coordinated with our dresses, and our dimes tied tightly in one end of a handkerchief, we would act grown up and go in by ourselves.” Linda Higgs also enjoyed the feeling of independence she got by going to the theater alone and spending some quality time with Elvis Presley. “I rode the bus downtown to see *Love Me Tender* five times a day on four occasions,” she said.

Vera Jameison and her friends went to the theater expressly to admire the dashing ushers. Visits to the theater completed their downtown window-shopping ritual.

> There were all those theaters downtown, but it was a big deal to go to the Tampa. It was a big part of our lives when I was in nurse’s training. When we got any time off, that was where we headed. There wasn’t much to do in that day and age, and it got my mind off work. I could walk the streets by myself, and I didn’t feel any danger at the theater. I would go there by myself.

Years after leading an elephant down Franklin Street, Colonel Tom Parker led his protégé to Tampa Theatre’s screen, drawing big crowds. 1956. *Tampa Tribune*.

As a smaller movie palace, Tampa Theatre lacked a nursery to supervise young children that might be found in larger houses. Still, it was not uncommon for working women to use theaters as day care surrogates. Only the presence and supervision of the ushers made this arrangement possible. Blondelle Gladney said, “You’d feel safe in there. Nothing went on crooked in that theater. The ushers watched everything; they were like hawks.” That went for children, too. “It was a safe place to put your kids,” she said. “This lady would drop her little kids off and say ‘Blondelle, I want you to take care of my little girls.’ I’d tell the ushers and they watched them.” Her coworker Maggie Radin recalled the same Tampa Theatre patron: “You know, we would take care of those kids all day long. One mother worked at the five-and-ten [store], and she would bring lunch to them. The kids would be with us for eight hours. That was kind of funny, we actually took care of children. We were their babysitters.”

Rituals and Romance

Rituals and romance have profound roles in the bonds between theater and patron. Anna and Lee Duncan were Tampa Theatre lifers who marked the stages of their lives at the palace. Lee Duncan set the stage by explaining,

> A family might have a radio, maybe. There was no such thing as TV. There was no place else to go. It wasn't the movies; it was a social event, going out on a Sunday. It was the thing for working people to be able to do. People worked six days a week, the only day off was Sunday, so everybody went there because that was the place to go. You always had a line waiting to get in on Sundays.

Anna Duncan also recalled the times.

> My family wasn't wealthy, but we found the money to go every Sunday to the Tampa Theatre. Mother, father, and myself. We went and it was something I grew into. It was something I did in high school on Friday nights because it was the only thing to do, really. It was really easy to get to. You could get any streetcar. Growing up, we watched anything on Sundays, and when I was going out with him [Lee] it was anything on Fridays. It really didn't make that much of a difference what the movie was. You may not have done much the rest of the week, but on Sundays we went to the Tampa Theatre all dressed up.

Lee concurred: "Oh yes, a coat inside at the Tampa Theatre."

Ellen Bardin recalled, "When you came to the theater you were dressed, no shorts or short sleeves. You wore Sunday clothes." Charles Bardin added, "Men wouldn't think of coming to the theater without a coat."

Nancy Dobson repeated a similar downtown ritual in the 1960s, with Tampa Theatre as the destination.

> That was the only place my mom would let me go because she knew the management would be watching us. I'd take the bus down to the Tampa Theatre. I always had pocket money, and I'd get all dressed up and just sit there hoping

At first, most movie palaces only offered candies and refused to sell lower-class snacks such as popcorn, which did not appear at the Tampa until the 1940s. Robertson and Fresh Photograph Collection, USF Digital Commons.

Film program manager James DeFord was hired as a concessionist in 2007. His future wife, Gina, started work the same week. They were married onstage in 2021 in a ceremony officiated by John Bell. James DeFord.

somebody would come say hello. That was really fun, the whole day would be taken up, the bus ride, the movie, and the ride back.

It had so much respect. The restrooms are so beautiful. I felt luxurious as if I were in a castle. The stars and the blackness of the sky made me feel like I was outside. The draperies, lights, statues, and sculptures made me think it was an opera house. It made me feel very special.

Mrs. Frank James remembered the first date with her future husband, when he invited her to a special New Year's Eve showing. "We sat in the balcony, and we were very dressed up," she said. "Around twelve o'clock the movie was interrupted for a few minutes of song and celebration. At midnight he kissed me. That was very unusual to have a kiss on the first date in those days. We were so happy that night."

Management was aware of the balcony's reputation as a romantic spot for couples. The farther back they sat, the more privacy couples had from anyone behind them. Small ads for special late-night showings suggested, "Let's make whoopee at the Tampa Theatre midnight show tonight."

From the projectionist's booth, it was common for personnel "to see them up there kissing and hugging" in the balcony, Gladney recalled. "Everybody wanted to be up on that balcony, you know. Anytime you saw a boy and a girl together, you knew they were going to the balcony. The ushers were always watching everybody."

Alex Hull recalled, "The usher was the king of the aisles, the cop on the beat and monitor of our morals while in the balcony." The ushers occasionally found good reasons to break the rules, Hull explained, such as on Saturday mornings, during shows for children, when "the balcony was closed so kids wouldn't run around up there, this usher would sneak me up there and he and I would smooch." Evelyn Salvatore said of the ushers, "They had to look good. I married one of them."

Theater Organ 101

When it comes to teaching the history and music of theater organs, there are few who can compare to Steven Ball, the artist in residence at Tampa Theatre. "I was always drawn to the organ," Ball said, "that combination of art, engineering, and music."

Ball explained how and why pipe organs became fixtures in deluxe movie palaces.

Tampa Theatre was born in the era of silent film, when live musicians provided the soundtrack. The Mighty Wurlitzer Theater Organ was a favorite of movie palaces. 1926. *Motion Picture News,* 1926. Internet Archive.

What we think of as the theater organ is a very specific machine that was designed for one purpose, which was the accompaniment of motion pictures. It's an immensely powerful and colorful machine that evolved over time.

Theaters grew in size very quickly. Once you get past a couple hundred seats, a piano, which was the usual form of accompaniment in the early years, couldn't move the air in the room. If the room was full, the piano would disappear. Organs were logical to put into these buildings. Theater organs were purpose built to be one-man theater orchestras. It was part of a whole explosion in the entertainment industry. The buildings themselves were evolving. There were over seven thousand theater organs installed in this very brief twenty-year window between about 1910 and 1930. The Wurlitzer company was the largest producer in their day, and in 1926, when Tampa Theatre was built, they were just about to enter their biggest year of production, when they produced an organ a day.

What you're looking at onstage is just the organ console. This is a control panel, the user interface, but the actual organ has all the pipes and the sound effects that are installed behind the walls of the theater. It's designed to be invisible because it is a supporting element. There are sixty-one keys on an organ keyboard. One pipe is assigned for every single note. There's sixty-one pipes in a rank. The other part is what we call the stops. That is each one of the members of the orchestra. In order to sound that pipe, I have to have one key depressed, and one stop engaged to turn another rank of pipes on. The keyboards are like different sections of the orchestra. We'll put the woodwinds over here, we'll put the brass on this keyboard, we'll have the strings down here. We're trying to think like a full orchestra.

We had a twenty-piece orchestra here, the largest in our theater district, and the organ worked in tandem with the orchestra. The reason for that was because we were open about twelve hours a day. A normal routine would be to have three complete shows, and so, the orchestra would play an overture, you'd have a short film, you could have vaudeville acts, you'd have a newsreel, and then you'd have a feature film. If you ask any musician to play twelve hours straight through, they're gonna drop dead on you.

The orchestras also needed to have somebody to double parts, because maybe the orchestra is missing a clarinet or, or a woodwind section, or violins, and you want to have a fuller sound. The organs could double all those parts at the same time. They could also take over for the orchestra when they needed a break.

These theaters were opening weekly. The Wurlitzer Company wasn't the only company installing organs. Many other companies were church organ builders who also produced organs for theaters. Every theater that had a new instrument needed to have a competent person playing. That could make or break the show. Because it's much more complicated than just scoring the film. You have to be able to work with an orchestra, do orchestration, read parts, transpose, improvise. The money was amazing. The starting salary at that time for a competent musician in a theater would have been about fifty bucks a week. All the way up to the most highly paid musician at the time, which was Jesse Crawford at the New York Paramount, and he made a thousand dollars a week plus his royalties and recording.

These were big investments. They spent the same amount of money in their time for these instruments that we would spend in a modern theater for surround sound. Everything was installed on a floor frame that's independent from the walls so it could be repossessed, because if it was screwed to the walls, it would become a fixture. In other words, many theaters were making payments on their instruments.

Eddie Weaver

Like the electric guitar, synthesizer, and autotuned vocal after them, the massive theater organs helped to define the eras in which they thrived. They lent an air of majesty to the pseudosacred proceedings of dream palaces. The music of organs, whether accompanied by an orchestra or played solo, was the keystone of the movie

Organist Eddie Weaver returned to Tampa Theatre for its grand reopening in 1977. Tampa Theatre.

palace experience before the age of talkies. The organists were often considered stars in their own right, almost as lofty as those on the screen. As a star, the organist needed to be able to project an energetic stage presence, excellent organ skills, and dynamic choir direction. Tampa Theatre kicked off with teenage Eddie Weaver as the featured organist. He was so important that he had a backup man, L. J. Pico, who was kept on call by Publix Theatres.

Weaver recalled his time at Tampa Theatre.

> I'd already done some playing in Florida, in Miami and Coral Gables. It all started when I left Eastman School of Music [in Rochester, New York] to play at a picture house in Batavia, New York. Somebody heard me and took me to meet Henry Murtagh, one of the great Wurlitzer men of that era. Murtagh taught me a lot. You see, playing the theater organ you are really in show business and he didn't just play, but had to do all these tricks. In time he introduced me to Boris Moros, the musical director of Paramount Pictures in New York. He hired me and sent me to Florida in 1926. I opened the Coral Gables

Theater and then went to play for a while at the Olympia in Miami until the big hurricane of 1926 hit. It tore the roof off the theater and blew my violin away—I used to play it as part of the act—and it got all my music as well.

I gave up and went back home to Pennsylvania. I'd been home about two hours when a call came through from Moros, "You've got to go back to Florida. You've got to open the Tampa Theatre." I did, and stayed six months. I especially like Tampa, a lot more than the Atlantic coast. It reminded me a little more of up north, I suppose. There were good people here too. One of my good buddies was Jack Hobby, the assistant manager of the theater. He was about my age and we both had money to spend. I was seventeen, I had a good salary, didn't have any income tax or withholding, so we really lived it up. We drove over to St. Petersburg just to use up gas. I was living in the Tampa Bay Hotel; that was a mighty plush place. You lived high on the hog there.

The theater was quite the glamorous spot in Tampa in those days. I guess that was true in a lot of communities. We got all dressed up in tuxedos, me and the theater managers and so forth. The ushers had snappy uniforms. The audiences were good at matinees and in the evenings, always pretty full houses. And they really got a good deal for their money. We had a good orchestra. John Ingram was the conductor. They started the show, playing for about twenty-five minutes. Then I'd start the picture and the orchestra would go out for a spell. Then they'd come back and we'd alternate until the picture was over.

One thing that was real popular was the [sing-along] slide songs. We didn't have any sound in those days of course, so when the song would start with a slide up on the screen that said something like, "All right, get ready to sing, Let's go!" Then there would be slides with the words to the song. "I'm Betting on You" was one of the first songs we did in Tampa. Real popular numbers in that era were "My Blue Heaven," "Baby Face," "Yes Sir, That's My Baby."

I was a little bitty kid playing a two manual organ with a big orchestra. Sometimes I was so sleepy I played with my elbow on my knee.

Beginning in 1937, Weaver performed in the theaters of Richmond, Virginia, for the next fifty years, including more than two decades at Loew's (today Carpenter) Theatre, an Eberson atmospheric that opened in 1928.

The Last Musician

Wurlitzer wunderkind Eddie Weaver might have stayed, but his heart told him to leave. He was in love with a cashier, his future wife, in Batavia, New York. He left Tampa after six months with fond memories. Weaver soon met Yale student Eddie Ford, who was playing at the Roger Sherman Theater in New Haven, Connecticut. Weaver talked Ford into applying for the organist seat at the Tampa. The twenty-year-old organist first performed at Tampa Theatre on May 1, 1927.

Charles Bardin recalled,

> Eddie Ford brought the house down because he was a real good organ player. He would play the popular tunes of the day and the words would be flashed on the screen. Can you imagine having a theater packed at three in the afternoon? That's how it was every day. There were special prices for schoolchildren, so the kids from Plant High School and Hillsborough High School and even the junior high schools would flock in here, and there would be a line up here by three. They let the kids in for twenty-five cents. The place would be packed, and of course they would really let out singing when he played.
>
> Sometimes he would play another number because he got such a hand from the kids. I'm a musician myself and I appreciated his talent. He played beautifully and he played the songs the young people wanted to hear. The truth is all the girls thought he was nice-looking. He never used sheet music. He had an incredible memory. They'd call out a song and he could play it. He was a showman while he was on stage, but he didn't have much personality while you were talking to him. He wasn't very personable.

In ads for the theater, small text below the feature read, "Cartoon, News, Eddie Ford." His expressive performances and sing-along slides served as attractions in themselves, becoming the subject of public discussion and argument. Letters to local newspapers engaged in a contentious debate about which songs were appropriate for the theater. The sensibilities of two generations of music fans vied for the spotlight as classical and jazz music collided in the public consciousness. Movie palaces themselves embodied the same conflicting impulses between tradition and modernity, aspirations to high culture and more popular tastes. Eddie embraced both.

For some in the audience, adjusting to the modern age proved difficult. One wrote to the *Tribune* in 1928, "I think Eddie would be all right if the management would allow him to play the good music of which he is capable, instead of requiring to do a lot of silly and meaningless stuff to accompany those ridiculous things [lyric slides] on screen. Cut out the clowning and let Eddie play real music."

"Mr. Ford is an artist," another letter read. "There is no doubt that popular music has the precedent over the more classical music among present-day audiences. At the same time, Mr. Ford knows that there are a great number of people who like the classics and the ballad type of number. So, to hit a happy medium, he changes around, constantly." Another reader put it more succinctly: "Perhaps we would prefer the classic music but who would applaud it?"

As a scholar of early cinema, theater operations manager Joey Hager provided insight.

> Newspaper reports would say, "The music program is worth the price of admission." Eddie Ford and John Ingram were vital to the success of the Tampa in the early days. While the movies often disappointed, the music never did. That level of artistry and dedication may be why John Ingram is said to have been the first theater orchestra leader given permission by Paul Whiteman to perform Gershwin's *Rhapsody in Blue*. Whiteman was very protective of that piece yet allowed Ingram to perform it. On Valentine's Day weekend 1927, it made its debut in Tampa as part of the program for Clara Bow's *It*.

On December 16, 1928, *Mother Knows Best* ushered in the age of talking pictures at Tampa Theatre. *Tampa Tribune*.

Ford left in 1928 just as the Tampa Theatre was transitioning into talkies and away from live music and silent films. If studios such as Paramount wanted to include music or vaudeville as part of their shows, they simply filmed live performances and sent the film reels on the road. Audio equipment was installed, and sound movies made their debut on December 16 with *Mother Knows Best*. Conductor Frank

The music of Eddie Ford attracted many devotees as the accompanist became an attraction in his own right. 1930. Robertson and Fresh Photograph Collection, USF Digital Commons.

Grasso, who replaced John Ingram, took the orchestra on a farewell tour of local venues before they were laid off. The same pattern played out across the country, with thousands of musicians out of work. Operations manager Hager said,

> We were not the first downtown theater wired for sound. That was the Victory [later renamed the Palace], when they premiered *When a Man Loves* in January of 1928. Tampa Theatre didn't get wired for sound until December of 1928, almost a full year after the Victory. We missed out on *Wings* and *The Jazz Singer,* but once we did have that system in place, the papers noted consistently that our system was far superior to what the Victory had. It was a quick transition, too. On a Saturday night, the orchestra accompanied Lilian Gish in *The Wind.* On Sunday morning, the orchestra was cleared out, and the talkies had taken over.

Musicians and their unions resisted the shift in entertainment and urged audiences to demand "living music" at the movies. The Musicians Association of Tampa, Local 721 of the American Federation of Musicians, staged movies with live bands in an attempt to sway public opinion. The Antonio López Orchestra played at Tampa Theatre for a week in 1930, inviting viewers to visit M. L. Price's music store nearby to vote for "living music, the only true form of musical enjoyment."

The studios and public learned to live without orchestras, but some organists remained at their posts. At the Tampa Theatre, the Wurlitzer is practically part of the building, and its sounds had become part of the experience there. Thanks in large part to Eddie Ford's recurring role as the wizard of the Wurlitzer, the organ remains a vital part of the Tampa Theatre today. After several stints in the 1930s, Ford left again in 1941, and people complained in letters to the newspapers. One wrote, "With Eddie Ford no longer at the console in the Tampa Theatre, the place loses the romantic atmosphere his music created there. It was Eddie's music that added the needed touch of fun and laughter to the theater." Another reasoned, "Many of us have been faithful customers of the Tampa Theatre, rather than the less expensive neighborhood theaters, solely because Eddie Ford's unfailingly fine music justified the higher admission. Without this feature, the Tampa loses its only distinction, and might as well cut its prices, run double bills, and put in a popcorn machine."

Much of Ford's absence was for a good cause. The musician served in the United Service Organization (USO) shows entertaining servicemen for five years. He returned to Tampa Theatre for his final residency in 1947.

Joe Paleveda remembered how Ford "would go down to the basement and get in the organ, flipping a little switch as soon as the newsreel was over. Ford announced through a microphone what song he would play as the opening number. Ford also had his own daily noontime radio show on WDAE and was somewhat of a local celebrity."

Elizabeth Finley said her brother, projectionist Fink Finley, sometimes deliberately diverted the spotlight off of Ford during his performances to irritate the prima donna. "He would bow to the audience and then he would come upstairs and bawl them out," she said. A longtime technician at the theater said of Ford, "When he would first get there, the music was kind of dull, but he would come down with a gallon of wine and as the wine disappeared from the jug, the arrangements got infinitely better."

Uncle Tom's Cabin

The Civil War and Jim Crow cast long shadows over the Sunshine State. The 1920s bore witness to horrific racial violence in a deeply segregated territory. Today, names like Rosewood and Ocoee are still seared into the consciousness of those who know what happened in those places. Membership in the Ku Klux Klan soared to new heights, and terrifying lynchings plagued the state. White-only and Black-only theaters were the norm across the South. Larger theaters might include a segregated entrance and seating section, typically in balconies, designated for dark-skinned patrons. Miami's Olympia Theater included a section for people of color. As a smaller movie palace for its time, Tampa Theatre was not designed to be segregated but opened as a White-only establishment.

While *Uncle Tom's Cabin* was denied a theatrical run, the film *Song of the South,* with more commercial appeal and a more sanitized depiction of the American South, played for a full week twenty years later. 1947. *Tampa Tribune.*

The janitorial staff were the only Black people allowed inside the building for close to forty years.

In 1927, the release of *Uncle Tom's Cabin* was a major event. It took two years and $2 million to produce the epic adaptation of the best-selling novel. The film, first released as a silent movie and later with sound, was noted for its strong performances, faithfulness to the novel, and what at the time were considered brutal depictions of slavery. To test the southern market, Universal Studios screened a milder edit of the film in St. Augustine. The response was positive but lukewarm. After its release in the fall of 1928, Atlanta, Birmingham, and Jacksonville banned the milder edit of the film for depicting slavery in a negative light.

The film's upcoming release elicited mixed reactions in Tampa, and Consolidated Amusements, owners of Tampa Theatre, were wary of courting controversy with the city's elite. Management stated that the picture would not be shown there if it was found to be "objectionable to Southern families." Tampa Theatre hosted a private screening of the controversial film for the United Daughters of the Confederacy and a group of influential men invited by Mayor D. B. McKay to determine its fitness for public consumption. A local journalist noted, "Synchronized with sound, and accompanied by a complete musical score, [the film] was condemned this morning by members of the United Daughters of the Confederacy and other club women as 'unequaled for sheer brutality and an insult to the South. It is a picture that should not be shown anywhere.'" A Mrs. Thompson said the picture was an affront to Southern womanhood as she defended her ancestors, insisting, "My grandmother refused to sell her slaves. She said she would as soon think of placing her children on the block."

The *Tampa Tribune* noted, "Members were unanimously agreed that it was a picture to spread hate, develop racial antagonism and revive the old feeling of sectionalism. Floggings, dogs attacking people, separations. Nothing has been left out in the way of cruelties. The picture is not only untrue. It is uncivilized, and it is unthinkable that producers are releasing it for showing anywhere." The *Tribune* summarized, "Asserting the film presented an untrue picture of Southern life and included atrocities that were unthought of in slavery days, members of the delegation and officials of the theater were unanimously against its public exhibition."

Accordingly, Consolidated Amusements banned the film at Tampa Theatre. The *Tampa Times* celebrated the decision. "That is a fine spirit," its editor wrote. "No doubt the Tampa Theatre would have had a good 'box' had it displayed this picture. [But it is] offensive to a considerable number of Tampans." The *St. Petersburg Times* was far friendlier to the film, giving it a sensational review. The *Miami Herald* called it "unexcelled."

While *Uncle Tom's Cabin* was withheld from Tampa Theatre, competition screened it elsewhere for capacity crowds. The new Park Theater in Hyde Park, Florida, part of the Southern Theater chain, resisted the complaints of City Councilman Sumter Lowry and Mayor D. B. McKay to cancel screenings of the film. J. T. Horne, the owner of the Park Theater, replied publicly,

> Without being rude, no one is compelled to see the picture who does not desire to do so, but frankly, we do not propose to be dictated to by a certain few people who may be prejudiced. We are catering to the masses, the theatergoers of this vicinity who want the opportunity of seeing this wonderful photo play which opportunity has been denied them so far in the city. About sixty other Florida towns and cities have endorsed and shown this picture. We want to give the public what they want.

The film was screened without incident for a week as planned. For the time being, Tampa Theatre bowed to the dictates of Dixie. The race riots in the wake of *Uncle Tom's Cabin* screenings never did materialize.

Hell Harbor

Tampa had its own brush with Hollywood in 1929. Director Henry King chose to film his next feature there. *Hell Harbor* was a "jungle picture" set in a pirate village. Shooting commenced in September 1929 and lasted just over three months. Based on *Out of the Night,* a novel by Rida Johnson Young, *Hell Harbor* was the first all-talking film made in Florida. It took seven freight cars to haul the bulky technical equipment from California.

Leading lady Lupe Velez, known as "The Mexican Spitfire," arrived by train to find Florida Governor Doyle Carlton waiting for her at the landing. She socialized at the Floridan Hotel during a reception and then took a jaunt to Plant Park, where a crowd of five thousand well-wishers pressed closer for a look at the starlet. "It makes the flesh goose pop out of my skin!" she quipped.

Velez's appearance that evening at the Tampa Theatre was good fun, with her

The production of *Hell Harbor* in Tampa raised hopes that the area might host more moviemaking in the future. 1930. Tampa Theatre.

IN GRATEFUL REMEMBRANCE OF TAMPA'S HOSPITALITY

Inspiration Pictures and the entire company of "Hell Harbor" will long remember the reception accorded them in Tampa, Florida.

For more than ten weeks every imaginable courtesy and kindness was shown us by people who had no other purpose but their inherent desire to make and keep us happy, in Tampa.

We were more than impressed by the fact that many courtesies were extended beyond the limit of our contractual obligations, which, in these days of feverish commercial enterprise, is something to be deeply appreciated.

It seemed at one time that it would be almost impossible for us to reciprocate, but we hope that what we have done in the way of publicizing our activities in Tampa, will in some measure make the people of Tampa believe that our appreciation has not been confined to verbalities.

We will not easily forget the patience, indulgence and activity of many of Tampa's prominent citizens on behalf of the "Hell Harbor" unit.

To Trenton C. Collins, Publicity Director of the Tampa Chamber of Commerce, the company wishes to express its gratitude for his indefatigable co-operation in the production of "Hell Harbor".

For their unlimited good will and helpfulness we want to offer our sincere thanks to Carl Brorein, President of the Chamber of Commerce; W. T. Williams, County Commissioner and Hal Thompson, Managing Director of the Floridan Hotel.

It would be a herculean task to thank the editors and publishers of Tampa's representative newspapers - The Times and Tribune - for their daily contributions and encouragement.

It is impossible to include the names of hundreds of others who made our stay in Tampa a memorable one, but let it be known that this general expression of our gratitude is none the less sincere.

All our good wishes and kind thoughts to Tampa and its people.

Henry King, Director
Inspiration Pictures, Inc.

GOVERNOR DOYLE E. CARLTON

CARL BROREIN

TRENTON C. COLLINS

MAYOR D. B. McKAY

W. T. WILLIAMS

HAL THOMPSON

singing, telling jokes, and impersonating starlets such as Gloria Swanson. A *Tampa Tribune* article on September 19, 1929, recapped her performance.

> [Velez] preened and strutted like a little peacock and had a grand time while a capacity crowd gave her a tremendous ovation. Lupe tripped around the stage like a schoolgirl just home from the classroom. She sang a bit of syncopated melody to accompaniment of an organ player, dragged Al St. John from the wings for an unmerciful mauling, made him delight the audience with a tap dance and comedy falls and wound up her act by kidding a bashful admirer.

The theater had just previewed director King's movie *She Goes to War,* also a Lupe Velez vehicle.

Seeking a sense of reality for the set, King and his studio, Inspiration Pictures, transformed Tampa Bay's Rocky Point into a Caribbean pirate community. Filming outside the confines of the studio system was rare at the time. King also recruited a variety of talent from Tampa to realize his vision. In a party scene, the Cuban *son* band Sextet Habanero played, and the dancers were all locals, including a real-life cook and a known smuggler. Local journalist Rondo Hatton, who became an actor specializing in horror films, also made an appearance.

On January 24, 1930, Publix-owned Victory Theater premiered *Hell Harbor* in a gala attended by Mayor D. B. McKay. Director Henry King said, "The eyes of movieland are on Tampa." The *Tampa Daily Times* reported, "Hollywood, New York, and now Tampa—the three names will be linked after tonight as world's Premier centers, where the new productions are thrown on the screen for the public's scrutiny for the first time. And as Tampa goes, says director Henry King, so goes the world."

Hell Harbor was received well nationally, but it failed to make much of a lasting impression. Tampa's moment in the sun proved short-lived. Before filming of *Hell Harbor* was complete, the stock market had crashed. No one could deny that trouble was in the air.

Depression

Tampa Theatre was built for the heady, hard-driving days of the 1920s, when getting rich seemed to be within anyone's reach, especially the Hollywood studio moguls. The Florida land boom redefined the state as a desirable destination for tourism and investment. Tampa was well positioned to ride the wave of prosperity that buoyed the state. The stars seemed to align sometime in the early 1920s, but just as quickly, the city's fortunes dimmed.

The first warning signs appeared before Tampa Theatre even opened. Deadly hurricanes lashed the state and sobered investors. Dark portents hit closer to home with the mysterious death of a well-known Tampa developer. The day before Tampa Theatre's opening, dashing real estate mogul D. P. Davis was declared missing at sea. Whether he'd fallen off a steamer or thrown himself into the ocean was up for debate. His doomed real estate empire and unusual departure were all the talk on opening night.

The worst came with the crash. In July 1929, six of Tampa's banks failed after rumors of insolvency, costing their clients $10 million. Several months later, while the *Hell Harbor* cast and crew were busily filming in town, a thunderclap on Wall Street was heard around the world. On Black Monday, October 28, 1929, skies darkened everywhere after the catastrophic stock market crash. It seemed as if the theater had joined the boomtime party just as it was breaking up.

Young Charles Bardin's career in the movie business illustrated its quickly changing fortunes. He joined Tampa Theatre as a teenage usher in 1929 after leaving high school to work in the theater business full time. He transferred between several theaters for broad experience across the Publix chain in Tampa. When he attained the position of assistant manager, his future seemed bright. Then the Depression changed everything. With more than 1,200 theaters, mostly in the Southeast and Texas, the mighty Publix theater chain crumbled when the Great Depression set in. It began selling off outlets in 1933 and ceased to exist in Florida shortly afterward. Jacksonville-based Sparks Theater Company bought most of the Publix Theatres empire, including the Tampa Theatre. When Bardin was demoted from manager to usher, he went back to high school and graduated a year late.

The land bust and Depression made themselves sorely felt across the social spectrum as Florida slipped back into poverty's slumber. In Tampa, the cigar industry's steep decline began after peaking in the mid-1920s. Depictions of smoking in Hollywood movies helped to popularize mass-produced cigarettes. The fortunes of Tampa as a whole were reflected in its annual building permits, which went from $2.6 million in 1920 to $23.4 million in 1925. In 1931, they had shrunk to just $409,000.

Charles Adler, founder of Bryn-Alan Photography in 1936, described Tampa's business district as a "ghost town" during summers.

I could have shot a cannon on Tampa Street all the way up to the Victory Theater and not hit a thing. The Florida land boom broke, and people lost their money. Everything had started with the boom. That was the beginning of history in Florida. It was like BC and AD. The Tampa Theatre became a marker of the boom. It was what was left of the superstructure that had fallen.

Bank Night

The Depression radically changed the calculus of the movie industry. Theaters struggled for a diminishing market as attendance shrank by a third. The mutual distress of the film industry and consumers gave rise to a national craze called Bank Night.

In 1931, theater booking agent Charles U. Yaeger increased attendance with lottery-style prizes, beginning in Colorado. In the typical practice of Bank Night, movie theaters raffled away prizes of money, products, or services to the cash-strapped public. To circumvent laws against gambling and lotteries, no purchase was required to write one's name into a theater's ledger and be eligible for a prize. Bank Night was a trademarked practice, so participating theaters signed on as franchisees to hold events of their own, paying fees between five and fifty dollars in proportion to their size.

When managers announced the chosen name in a drawing, the winner had five minutes to claim the prize, keeping contestants waiting close by. While staff called the winning name from the theater's stage, another employee with a bullhorn announced it to the milling crowd around the box office. Bank Night's prizes often began at one hundred dollars and increased if none was awarded the week before. Smaller prizes were also awarded in subsequent drawings. Occasionally the contest included prizes supplied by sponsors, a car, a radio, a refrigerator or stove, or even a paid vacation.

In 1934, the Bank Night craze struck Tampa. Five theaters signed on to hold weekly events on the day of their choice. Tampa Theatre's management chose Fridays for its drawings. The crowds appeared faithfully every Friday, and it had nothing to do with the film. Joey Hager, the theater's operations manager and programming historian, said, "People weren't necessarily coming into the theater on Bank Nights. They were getting their ticket and they were finding out if they won ten bucks, or a hundred bucks, or a bag of groceries, or a box of dishes. It didn't matter what was playing."

Projectionist Joe Paleveda recalled, "When they didn't have Bank Night there

The promise of prizes on "Bank Night" transfixed the cash-strapped public during the Great Depression, clogging the sidewalk and street with crowds every Friday. 1931. Courtesy of Tampa-Hillsborough County Public Library System.

wasn't much business." Tampa Theatre usher Bardin said of the Depression, "You can't imagine how terrible it was. I was a kid in the thirties, and I was making ten dollars a week. That was more money than three married men with families who lived on my street. Even doctors made sure they went to Bank Night. My wife would go to the dentist and ask him if he was going."

Seventeen-year-old Doris Keating saw *It Happened One Night* with a date at Tampa Theatre on an unforgettable Bank Night.

> I won one of the cash prizes—ten dollars—it was an enormous amount of money for me at the time. I was too exhilarated with my new riches to be considerate and invite my date to share refreshments after the show. I selfishly spent the entire ten dollars on myself. Incidentally, my date did ask me to accompany him again the following week, so I must assume he was not too unhappy with my selfishness. I don't recall much about the movie and I have not seen it since, but I do remember the night and my luck at the beautiful and unique Tampa Theatre.

Bank Night produced just as many memories of disappointment. Charles Adler recalled the experience of a family member who lost out on twenty-five dollars. He explained, "One night she was supposed to be at the theater, but she was out playing mischief somewhere else. Her name was called and everyone scattered like the wind looking for her. It would have been a tremendous bonus. Her family was in financial straits at the time."

The popularity of Bank Night led to its downfall. In cities across the country, throngs of people crowded downtown sidewalks and spilled out into the streets outside theaters, disrupting traffic and endangering the public. City officials sparred with theater owners over Bank Night practices and public safety. Tampa Theatre's management resisted using alternative ways to announce winners that would not require players to loiter nearby. For a while, police officers closed Franklin Street to traffic in front of the theater to accommodate the crowds. Similar stories played out everywhere, and in 1936, city and state governments increasingly viewed the practice as a nuisance rather than an innocent diversion. After years of legal skirmishing, Florida courts declared Bank Night illegal in January 1939.

The show began on the sidewalk, grabbing attention by creating a spectacle that included a stage with models atop the marquee. 1933. Robertson and Fresh Photograph Collection, USF Digital Commons.

The Exploitation Manual

Theater owners across the country resorted to every conceivable novelty to attract attendance. The *Film Daily Year Book of Motion Pictures* published an annual "Exploitation Manual" with a long list of promotional gimmicks, tie-ins, games, stunts, and themes to add some spice to what were usually trivial films.

Some of the most engaging campaigns enlisted local Hollywood hopefuls in a variety of entertainment roles and contests. The Charleston was all the rage in 1926. The theater held a contest featuring the dance onstage. At just eleven years old, Minnie Starling Johnson danced "like mad" with all the grown-ups. "It was the most wonderful night of my life because I won," she beamed years later. "The prize was three dollars, which back then bought a week's worth of groceries."

The theater held a contest for young women in Florida to win a spot in a stage revue dedicated to the glories of the Sunshine State. Adele Fitzgerald was one of eight young ladies chosen from Tampa, Jacksonville, Daytona Beach, and St. Petersburg. Recruited through local beauty contests, the winners rehearsed the show for six months and toured Publix theaters around the state.

Management found multiple ways to engage with the public and generate business. The ladies of the Junior League played bridge and sipped tea on the mezzanine before regularly scheduled matinees. Every Wednesday and Friday there were twelve tables in play, populated by women with influential names. The ladies played for bragging rights in the local newspaper, which featured winners in small articles every week. Mother's Day and Father's Day were obvious occasions for parental promotions. The United Daughters of the Confederacy organized free screenings for the dwindling numbers of Southern veterans.

Management offered matinees specifically for children on Saturday morn-

Miss Florida 1930, Margaret "Mickey" Ekdahl, modeled for the Publix theater chain's promotions. Tampa Theatre.

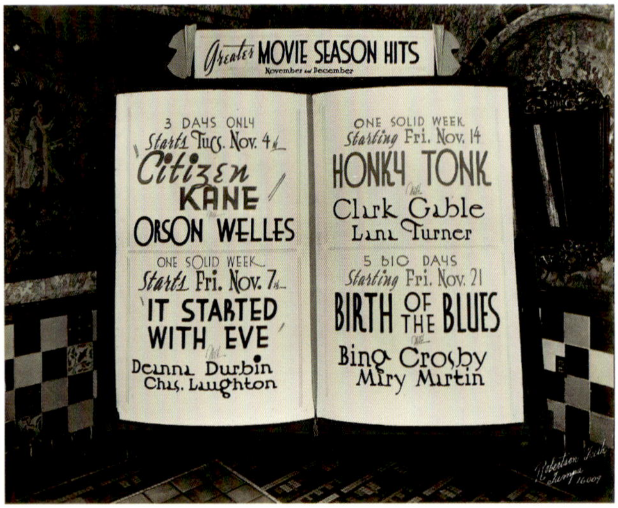

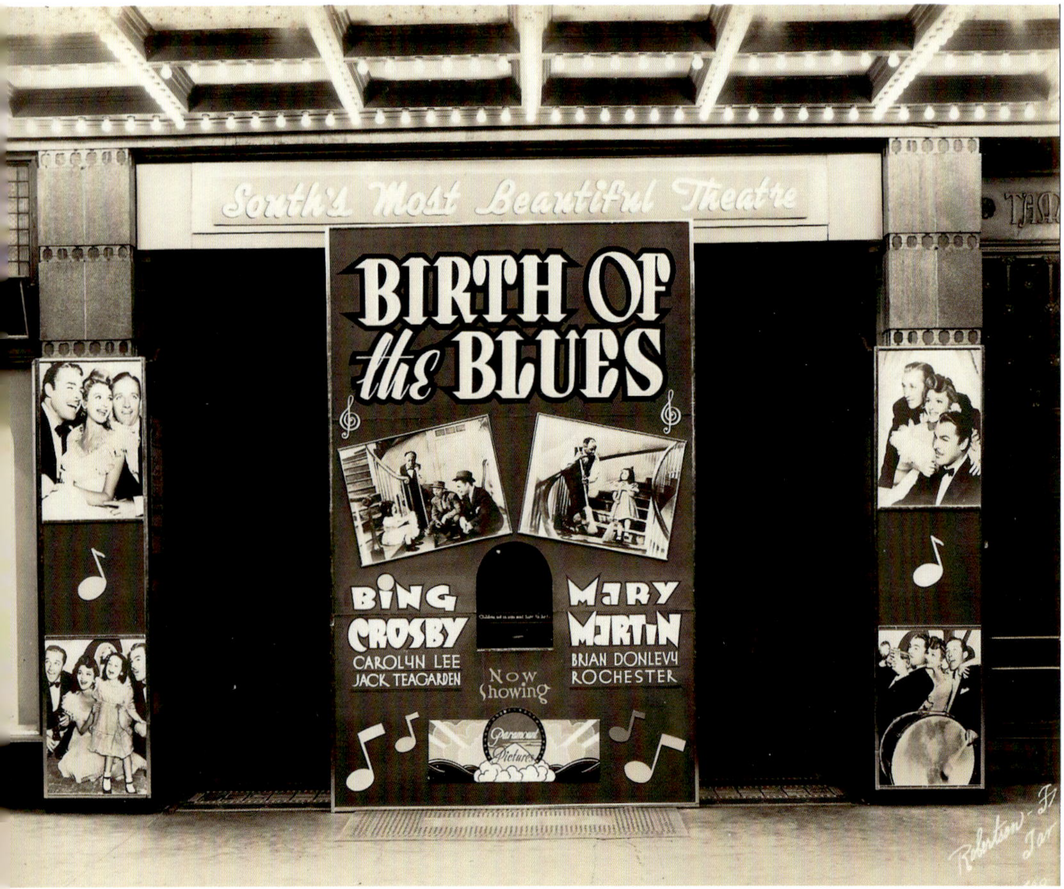

Big films came with elaborate promotional materials, often covering the box office and parts of the lobby. *left* The displays for *Birth of the Blues* in 1941 were extensive. Tampa Bay History Center. *above* Courtesy of Tampa-Hillsborough County Public Library System. *top left and right* Tampa Bay History Center.

To promote the Clara Bow film *Love among the Millionaires* in 1930, Tampa Theatre management partnered with a local beauty parlor to provide her signature haircut for patrons. Tampa Theatre.

Promotion of movies and products went hand in hand. A cane syrup display in the lobby coincided with screenings of the comedy *Honey* in 1930. Tampa Theatre.

Fred and Ginger led the celebration of a decade of movies on Franklin Street in 1936. *Tampa Tribune.*

ings. They worked with parent-teacher associations and the Boy Scouts to plan wholesome programming. A typical show might kick off with some "Our Gang" comedies and feature *The Rough Riders* (the 1928 sound version). In another promotion, the theater invited the mothers of Tampa to bring their babies to Plant Park's bandshell. There, a *Tampa Times* camera crew filmed the children to be featured in special all-Tampa newsreel supplements. Participants could see their children on the silver screen later in the week before the featured film.

To promote one of Clara Bow's films, *Love among the Millionaires* (1930), hairdressers offered bobbed haircuts in the lobby inspired by the "It" girl. The theater hired a soda jerk to sling drinks from a temporary bar for roadhouse night. To publicize a movie about crime and gambling, the lobby had a display of paraphernalia that had been confiscated from local gambling houses.

Product tie-ins were especially popular. For the movie *Honey* (1930), a booth was set up in the lobby offering free samples of Pure Gold Georgia Cane Syrup, a sweet product that promised to build strength. Crosley Radios from Jackson Furniture Companies graced the lobbies so everyone could get a good look at the latest models. Miss Florida modeled in a fashion review sponsored by Maas Brothers. Firestone Tires and their local service stores sponsored a screening of *Burning Up* (1930), a movie that promised romance and speed.

To take the message to the streets, Tampa Theatre dropped vouchers across the city from an airplane. Each free ticket was designed to look like a medieval herald scroll. Of course, most of the leaflets were worthless, with few winners scattered among them.

Street Scenes

Theater managers were well versed in the art of making a scene outside to draw attention. In 1930, the promotion for a movie called *Street Scene* provoked a scene of its own. On the tenth floor of the Citizens Bank building (Franklin and Zack Streets), a performer placed a mannequin in the top-story window as if it was a person intent on jumping. With sirens wailing, a fire truck rushed down Franklin and stopped below the would-be suicide while firemen prepared to catch him with a jumping sheet. Onlookers from nearby offices and stores emptied onto the street to watch the spectacle unfold.

Charles Bardin recalled,

> The whole corner was jammed up with people when they saw the fire truck come. I came running up and I saw this guy waving his hands. Of course, they were working all of this from the back. It looked like it was a real person and the crowd just got enormous. They let this thing go and the fireman purposefully let the dummy hit the street. Women fainted and screamed. No kidding, I nearly had a heart attack. I had no idea that this was just a sham, an advertisement. They let this big flier [banner] down that covered four floors and it said, "Street Scene at the Tampa Theatre." People were outraged because they thought they had witnessed a man committing suicide.

Sadly, in the throes of the Great Depression, it was all too believable that a ruined businessman might jump from an office tower.

Before becoming the manager of Elvis Presley, "Colonel" Tom Parker was a carnival booster and showman. He was Tampa's municipal dog catcher for a time and did some promotional work for the theater. Box office manager Blondelle Gladney remembered Parker's stint there: "It was during the Depression days, and money was hard to get. He made a dollar a day." Parker could often be seen walking Franklin Street leading an old bear or a lion to advertise a movie. He worked a summer

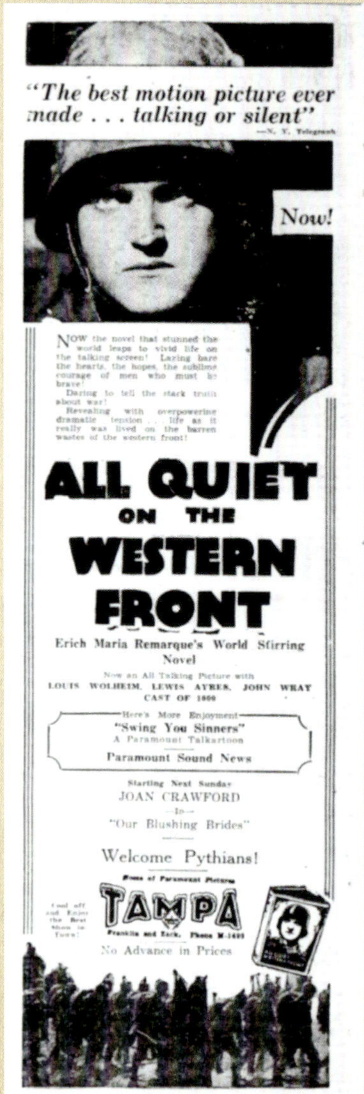

"The best motion picture ever made . . . talking or silent"
—N. Y. Telegraph

Now!

NOW the novel that stunned the world leaps to vivid life on the talking screen! Laying bare the hearts, the hopes, the sublime courage of men who must be brave!

Daring to tell the stark truth about war!

Revealing with overpowering dramatic tension . . . life as it really was lived on the barren wastes of the western front!

ALL QUIET ON THE WESTERN FRONT

Erich Maria Remarque's World Stirring Novel

Now an All Talking Picture with
LOUIS WOLHEIM, LEWIS AYRES, JOHN WRAY
CAST OF 1000

Here's More Enjoyment
"Swing You Sinners"
A Paramount Talkartoon

Paramount Sound News

Starting Next Sunday
JOAN CRAWFORD
—In—
"Our Blushing Brides"

Welcome Pythians!

Home of Paramount Pictures
TAMPA
Franklin and Zack.

No Advance in Prices

The street scene to promote *All Quiet on the Western Front* in 1930 included a mock military formation and a large sign on the box office that read "cooled by refrigeration." Tampa Theatre.

promotion walking the sweltering sidewalks dressed as Santa Claus. Parker led a pachyderm down Franklin Street to promote the film *Elephant Boy* (1937), starring India-born lead Sabu Dastagir. Gladney described the street scene with Parker and the elephant.

> He tied the elephant to the box office one day while he went in to use the restroom. The old elephant doo-dooed near the box office, and some lady slipped on it, and my gosh she was so mad she said she was going to sue the theater. She wanted to talk to the manager. Everyone around the theater was just dying laughing. From then on, I said "Don't you leave that elephant tied to the box office again!"

When Bank Night was banned in 1939, other giveaway promotions took its place. In 1941, 7-Up soft drink sponsored a game show on WDAE radio that offered various prizes, including six-packs of the beverage. Tampa Bay History Center.

A Florida-centered vaudeville revue produced by Publix Theatres held auditions at the Tampa Theatre before embarking on a nationwide tour. Adele Fitzgerald represented Tampa. 1928. *Tampa Tribune*.

Entertainment of all sorts enticed audiences to visit the theater. 1941. *Tampa Tribune*.

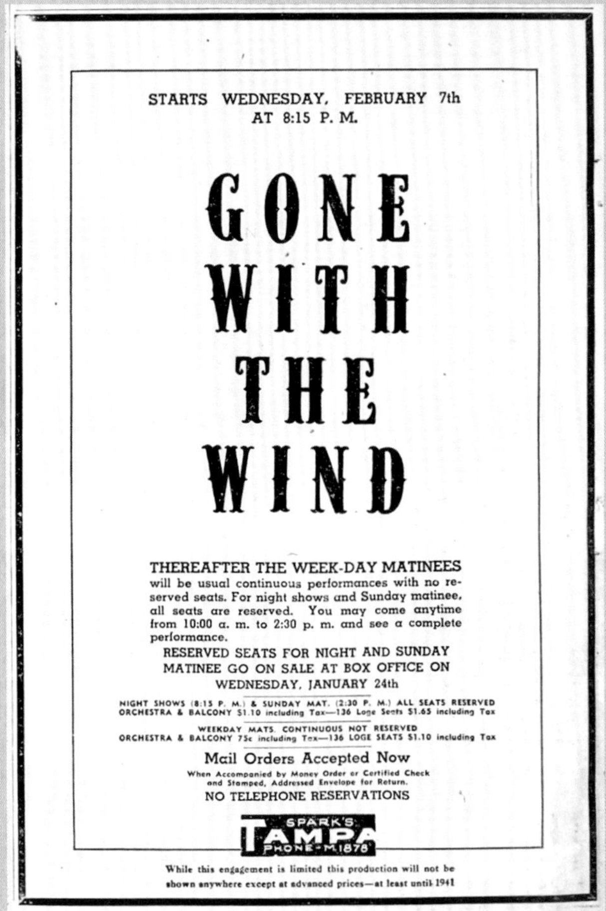

Gone with the Wind arrived in Tampa to much fanfare, reportedly re-creating the presentation it received at its Atlanta premiere. Blondelle Pate Gladney organized the reserved seating for the event. 1940. *Tampa Tribune*.

Every year, someone watches *The Wizard of Oz* for the first time at Tampa Theatre. In 1939, it was all of Tampa, in an exclusive premiere engagement. *Tampa Tribune.*

Walt Disney's short films were already a Tampa Theatre mainstay when his first feature-length film debuted there in 1938. *Tampa Tribune.*

Movies dominated the theater's schedule, but live music was still a feature on occasion. Paul Whiteman brought his danceable jazz to the stage in 1941. *Tampa Tribune.*

The street scenes continued well into the 1940s. Maggie Radin was a promotional model, usherette, and candy clerk for Florida State Theaters. She first came to the theater in 1940 when her family moved to Tampa from Virginia. "When I came to town, people told us all about the Tampa Theatre," Radin said. "The first time I saw it I thought it was just gorgeous. The blue sky with the stars—it just took my breath away." At age seventeen, she worked for the Strand Theater as an usherette and candy clerk. She augmented her pay (which was much lower than her male counterparts') modeling for department stores and theaters. For Greer Garson's *Julie Misbehaves* (1948), Radin wore a special form-fitting suit while cavorting in a bathtub. She stood backlit behind a curtain looking as if she wore nothing. She could hear onlookers wonder aloud, "Does she have anything on?" She acted out the scene three times a day for the week that the movie ran.

Rosalie Holland Stribling, a high school senior and part-time Tampa Theatre box office cashier, also participated in several theater promotions as a model. She reveled in her role. "A line would form around the block just to buy tickets to get in. Well, being seventeen, sitting in that booth gave me this feeling of such importance that I would have worked there for nothing," Stribling said.

Seasons Greetings
KRESS
J. J. NEWBERRY CO.
BOYDS
TAMPA
FLORIDA
Walk-Over SHOES
KINNEY
Burgert Bros
HOUSE of PHOTOGRAPHY

Franklin Street in 1941. With the Depression passed, it felt like downtown was on the rebound. Tampa Bay History Center.

3

War

In the late 1930s, the Great Depression finally lifted, only to give way to a new threat. After two decades of relative peace, the United States began to rearm as the international situation deteriorated. As war engulfed Europe and Asia, Florida bristled with a renewed military presence. In 1939, the Army established MacDill Air Base on Catfish Point just south of Tampa. Local shipyards ramped up production. Thousands of military and industrial personnel streamed in, and the city roared back to life. Downtown resumed its place as the center of commerce and retail activity.

In August 1941, the United States had not yet entered World War II when the British vessel *Oakworth* docked at Tampa. Gunner J. Tom Steele loved his stopover in the city. "I had a wonderful time in Tampa," he recalled. "The hospitality we received from the people was wonderful. The experience of the city is one of many happy memories." He avoided the two brothels that seemed to operate quite openly at the time. He mistakenly sat in the "colored" section of a streetcar, and a Black woman nearby suggested he find a different seat closer to the front.

For Steele, the highlight was visiting Tampa Theatre.

> We had to go into the balcony in the cinema. When we were waiting to be shown to our seats, we looked up and saw the black sky full of brilliant, jeweled glittering stars. One of the lads in a loud voice said, "The cinema ain't got a roof on! What are we going to do if it rains?" Then someone in the balcony shouted, "English sailors!" Looking over the balcony and down into the ground stalls, we saw everyone stand up and turn around, looking up at us and waving and cheering. What a thrill we had—it set the heart beating faster.

Tampa's solidarity with the British war effort against Nazi Germany and its menacing U-boats was loud and clear and foreshadowed US entry into the war that December.

Doris Whitaker remembered hearing the news on December 7, 1941, when the

Florida State Theatres joined the war effort with sly advertisements for its films. 1941. *Tampa Tribune.*

Soldiers march by Tampa Theatre during World War II. 1942. Tampa Bay History Center.

Japanese Imperial Navy bombed Pearl Harbor. "Going to the movies at the Tampa Theatre was my special treat," she said. "It's funny how something will stay in your heart and mind for years. I've always loved that theater." While she dreamed of dancing like Ginger Rogers, a military officer interrupted the film onstage. In a stern voice, he advised citizens not to be alarmed while he ordered all military personnel to immediately report to their posts. Whitaker said, "I have always remembered the goosebumps and the cold feeling I had that day."

Hollywood Upheaval

An interesting but largely unspoken aspect of the early moviegoing experience was that the bulk of the films were destined to be ephemeral. Movies were only as good as they needed to be. The reels might be screened for a few weeks at various theaters and quickly forgotten by those who made and watched them. Movie monopolies

Portions of this film were shot at MacDill Air Force Base and Al Lang Field and catered by the Columbia Restaurant. It held its southeastern US premiere at Tampa Theatre, with Mayor Hixon and MacDill officers in attendance. 1955. *Tampa Tribune*.

Manager O. G. Finley participated in an age-old theater marketing tactic: the public "apology" for not urging everyone to see that week's great new picture, *Miracle on 34th Street,* in the summer of 1947. *Tampa Tribune*.

Alongside a film that dramatized the transition from silent to talking films that Tampa Theatre experienced, the theater presented its first Wurlitzer concert in five years and a Tom and Jerry cartoon. 1952. *Tampa Tribune*.

like Paramount prioritized quantity over quality, producing frothy features of little consequence to keep earning profits every week. For every memorable classic, there were at least a hundred cheap, interchangeable duds destined for the dustbin of history. Movie palaces were meant to draw customers when quality films could not. In the large territories of theater chains such as Publix, there never seemed to be any consistent programming strategy except to keep all of the theaters running. Joey Hager explained,

> When you go through Tampa Theatre's program history, you might come across one week where the Palace is showing something like *A Streetcar Named Desire,* a film that you would expect would have played here. But we were playing some nonsense, nothing film. Because they had to kind of share the wealth. There didn't really seem to be much of a rhyme or reason. We didn't play a Chaplin film. We didn't play a Buster Keaton film. We were the Harold Lloyd house. Another theater had all the Chaplin films; another theater had all the Keaton films.

Most vintage movies were forgettable for their plots and productions and were entirely forgotten after their brief moment on the screen. The film that opened

Specialized newsreels allowed guests to see Tampa's Gasparilla Parade like never before. 1948. *Tampa Tribune.*

Gloria Swanson appeared on Tampa Theatre's screen from the silent era through her lauded performance as Norma Desmond. 1950. *Tampa Tribune.*

Alfred Hitchcock redefined the culture of movie theater attendance with one decree: "No one will be seated in the last ten minutes" of the film. 1958. *Tampa Tribune.*

Tampa Theatre, *The Ace of Cads,* is no longer in existence. That the film is now lost to history should come as little surprise. It is estimated that 90 percent of films shot in the United States before 1929 have not been preserved and will never be seen again.

The Hollywood studio system was all-powerful but also proved to be its own worst enemy. With a monopoly on every aspect of the business from top to bottom, the studio moguls couldn't resist using their influence to squeeze competition with unfair practices. The federal government had been pursuing antitrust litigation against the studio system for years. In 1948, a Supreme Court decision against Paramount broke up the entire Hollywood studio system. The reckoning came at a vulnerable time for the industry, with television coming into the marketplace. Ten years after the studio-theater breakup, the number of regular moviegoers declined by almost half. The golden goose that produced Tampa Theatre was no more.

For lifelong pals Donald Booth (*left*) and Jimmy Miller, their memories as Tampa Theatre ushers are treasured. Courtesy Donald Booth.

Goofing at the Movies

Donald Booth and Jim Miller grew up in Tampa and struck up a close friendship during the fourth grade. By the time they were teens in the 1960s, downtown Tampa had fallen on hard times, but Tampa Theatre still showed films and hired young workers.

Donald Booth described his luck in getting a job at the theater.

> I think I was in the ninth grade working at a carwash or something, and I was looking to better my career. It was definitely a cool job. I came down and applied and realizing they were hiring more people, my buddy, my partner in crime, I let him know about it. The best part about it was, like on Friday night, even though we weren't bringing our dates in and stuff, all our friends were. So, you can treat them nice and find them a seat. It had a wee bit of an esteem to it, being an usher.

Jim Miller was the friend Booth brought into the theater job. Miller recalled,

> One thing I remember was back then, when they showed a movie, they had boxes and boxes of reels. Some of the longer movies, there'd be four or five of these, big cassettes, and of course they didn't have an elevator that went up to the projection booth. I used to dread it, carrying those things up the stairs. They must have weighed sixty pounds each.

Movie palaces initially were considered too cultured to serve vulgar popcorn and other popular snacks. Tampa Theatre employed candy girls from the beginning but did not incorporate popcorn until the 1940s. By the time Booth and Miller arrived, the concession stand also served hot dogs and full-sized pickles. Booth described the variety of offerings.

> I remember all the box candies, the Jujubes, the bonbons, Raisinets, the popcorn. I for one could not resist the hot dogs, and I didn't pay for them. The old-fashioned ["bubbler"] juice machines, they were transparent. You'd fill the juice up and then it'd come down. They kept the balcony shut but when they had big showings, they would open it. Well, they had the concession upstairs running and then they shut the balcony down but they left that grape juice machine going. It was up there for like a month, and we said, "I wonder what that stuff tastes like?" Well, it had fermented into wine, so me and Rene Rodriguez drank the whole thing. We were a couple loaded ushers that day.

Booth and Miller reminisced about an especially memorable event at the theater.

> BOOTH: One of the funnest films was *Help!* by The Beatles. I remember we got down early Saturday morning, and the girls had been sleeping out along the sidewalk. It was wild.
>
> MILLER: When it got close to the doors opening, everybody was holding the doors [shut] and the girls were trying to get in.
>
> BOOTH: After I watched it three or four times, there was a part of the film where they're going, "Where's the ring?" It's like about three minutes into the film, "Who's got the ring?" Then all of a sudden, the camera goes on Ringo and it's the ring on his finger. And then the song "Help!" comes in and the girls just, well [went wild].
>
> I used to go behind the screen. It was up on these two-by-fours, and you could look through the screen, there's a million dots. I knew right when that scene was going to be, when Ringo would show, and I watched

Beatlemania arrived at Tampa Theatre with the Fab Four's first film release in 1964. More followed. *Tampa Tribune.*

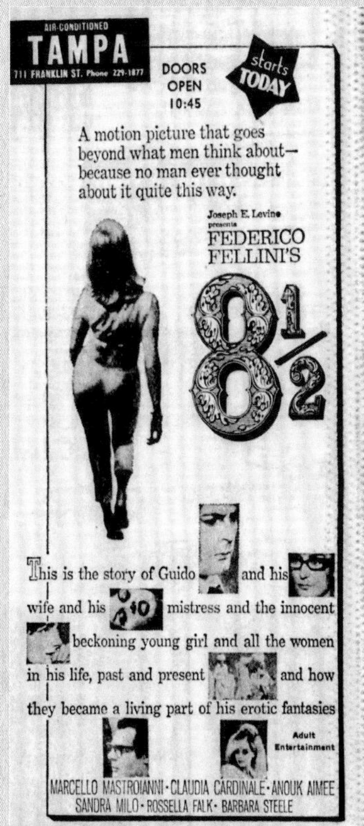

Films like Federico Fellini's *8½* signaled a change in Tampa Theatre's programming, which had been exclusively Hollywood fare for nearly forty years. 1963. *Tampa Tribune.*

Tampa's residents were introduced to 007 under the starry sky of Tampa Theatre when *Dr. No* premiered in an exclusive engagement in 1963. *Tampa Tribune.*

that front row [of girls react]. That had a little effect on me too. I ended up playing drums for fifty years, Ludwigs just like Ringo's. That was the closest I got to live Beatlemania.

MILLER: As far as being a single guy, it was like you died and went to heaven.

More Than a Porter

At Tampa Theatre, the only positions open for people of color were janitorial staff. In 1932, George Richardson took a job as janitor at the Walgreens in downtown Tampa and married Mae Young. "I was making $12.50 a week and that was pretty good back then," he remembered. Soon after, when Tampa Theatre needed to replace its original porter, Albert Sanchez, Richardson applied. He was offered fifteen dollars a week, and Mae soon joined him as a maid. Both were known for their meticulousness and dedication to their jobs. They were the only Black people allowed in the theater for much of its working life.

George may have been assigned an unglamorous role as Tampa Theatre's longtime janitor, but like Blondelle Gladney in the box office, he transcended his job, and his personality became part of downtown Tampa's pantheon. Maggie Radin recalled, "George was always at the Tampa as far back as I remember. He's part of that theater. He could run the theater as good as any manager could. He ordered the candy during the intermissions, then swept and straightened the bathrooms."

Gladney remembered a time when a patron lost his false teeth while screaming during a movie. "George Richardson found the damn teeth. He was the best porter we ever had," she said. Evelyn Salvatore remembered that the theater was always "spotless, everything had to be good and polished." Management "thought the world of George," but he and Mae had no chance of advancement. Still, compared to their other options in segregated Tampa, the theater job had comparably good pay and working conditions.

During World War II, Richardson joined the Marines and served in the Pacific. After the war, he and his brothers-in-law built his family home on Arch Street. Mae quit her job at the theater to raise their daughter, Pamela. George Richardson augmented his pay as a window washer downtown, spending most of his time on Franklin Street. "I like being on the street the best because you can meet more people that way," he said.

Tampa Theatre assistant manager Frank Connors said, "If George were to run

Franklin Street Fixture

He'll Retire From Downtown Duty

By JOHN ROBINSON

One of the few "fixtures" of old downtown Tampa will go the way of the wooden sidewalks and brick streets at the end of this year.

At 68, George Richardson is ready to put down the mop and broom and take his first vacation since he was in military service in 1946.

"Ol' George," as the shopowners call him, has cleaned store lobbies and windows for most of the small shops on Franklin Street for the last 20 or more years. He is not sure of the date because, as he puts it, "I've worked downtown all my life."

Richardson got his first downtown job in 1932 when he took on the job of janitor at the Walgreen's downtown.

"I was making $12.50 a week and that was pretty good back then," he said.

THEN, IN 1933, he was offered $15 a week as a janitor at the Tampa Theatre next door. He took the job and stayed there until he decided to go on his own, washing windows for the shops on Franklin Street.

"I liked being on the street the best because you can meet more people that way," Richardson said. And anyone who shops downtown knows that the friendliest person on the street is the tall, slender man behind the yellow wash bucket, with the words: "Caution — Wet" written on the side.

Dressed neatly in gray knit pants and white short-sleeved shirt, Richardson recalls the time when people used to come to town to do all their shopping.

"You used to have to walk on the sidewalk just like you were driving a car by walking on the right side of the sidewalk. It's not like that now; people just don't come to town much anymore," he said.

A NORMAL workday for Richardson begins at 4 a.m. He usually gets downtown around 5 a.m. to wake the bums and drunks and send them on their way.

"I usually have to chase them out of the store lobbies with my broom," he said. His day ends around 5 p.m. when he goes home and, in his words, "really begin to work."

Having been happily married for 43 years, Richardson knows that a husband's work isn't done until he goes to bed. His wife, Mae Young, used to work with him as a maid at the theater. She quit to raise their daughter, Pamela, who just graduated from Emory University.

Almost everyone downtown knows George Richardson, and most call him by name. As Frank Connors, assistant manager at the Tasmpa Theater, puts it: "If George were to run for City Council, he would have the vote of everyone in town — just on his honest reputation."

RICHARDSON RECALLS once when his honest reputation got him out of trouble with the police. Early one morning, he had gone downtown as he usually does. As a light drizzle started coming down, he stepped inside a store lobby to keep dry. Two men, standing in the corner, approached him and asked if he wanted to buy a couple of "numbers." Richardson, knowing that they meant they were selling bolita, replied "no." At that moment, two policemen walked up and arrested all three on a charge of selling bolita. When he was brought for a plea hearing, Judge Bob Johnson, who had worked as the doorman at the Tampa Theater years ago, recognized him.

Hearing Richardson's story Johnson dismissed the charges, saying "this man could never do any wrong, even if he tried."

The Richardson plans to travel around the United States after he retires. He says he hasn't left Tampa since he finished his stint in the service.

"I've worked all my life and feel I deserve a vacation with my wife, he said. "I've never even seen the college my daughter graduated from."

So when 1975 is over, one more thing will be gone from Franklin Street along with the streetcars, brick streets, wooden boardwalks, and shell-bed roads — a friendly, familiar face.

John Robinson is a free-lance writer and student at The University of South Florida.

Photos By
Dan Fager

George Richardson has been a Franklin Street fixture for more than 20 years, and shop owners will miss him when he retires. To regular downtowners, he's that familiar face who keeps windows and storefronts tidy and always has a friendly hello for passersby.

George Richardson served as the theater's porter for much of his life and was a friendly fixture downtown. 1975. © Tampa Bay Times/ZUMA Press.

Tampa's Black moviegoers were limited to Black-only theaters such as the Carver, which opened on North Boulevard in 1949. Tampa Bay History Center.

for City Council, he would have the vote of everyone in town just on his honest reputation." Shop owners who needed to step out for lunch or an errand often left George in charge of their businesses. His niece Sylvia Jean Dickens said, "They'd leave Uncle George in charge because they trusted him more than their own salespeople."

Richardson retired in 1975 at age sixty-eight. It would be his first vacation since 1946, when he was discharged from the military. He said, "I've worked all my life and feel I deserve a vacation with my wife. I've never even seen the college my daughter graduated from [Emory]." After his death in 1997, his friend James D. Marshall Jr. said, "He never wrote a book, but he was really a historian of downtown. He could tell you some stories. He was a storehouse of information, but that's all gone now."

Desegregation

In segregated Tampa, Black residents could see movies at Black-only theaters such as the Lincoln or Carver. Lifetime Tampa resident Darryl Miles remembered, "My mother told us that Black people could only go to the Lincoln Theater. It was dirty. It had a balcony and you could see big rats running across the screen."

Segregation seemed so entrenched as a public and private practice that it was difficult to imagine anything else. As a child, Rowena Brady was not especially concerned about segregation and the everyday racism that prevailed in Tampa at the time.

Some said that Tampa Theatre's best marketing was the cool, dry air spilling out its doors that could be felt on Franklin Street and from the streetcar stop nearby. For Black pedestrians during the days of segregation, feeling that air was a cold reminder of their lower status. 1941. Tampa Bay History Center.

> We didn't worry about it as kids growing up because the fights, civil rights, and everything hadn't come about yet. My dad provided well for his family. We had just about everything we wanted. You just didn't go to the Tampa Theatre. We couldn't go there, and we didn't worry about it. The best part of going downtown and passing by was the cool air that came out of that theater. It was air-conditioned. We wondered why in the world we couldn't have a show like that. It was so cool. We didn't know how it was inside because we were never allowed to go in, but we always felt that cool air.

As sit-ins took place at Woolworth's across the street in 1963, civil rights activists picketed outside what was then a whites-only Tampa Theatre. © Tampa Bay Times/Zuma Press.

Later, when Brady went downtown as a mother, she became more aware of the daily indignities of Jim Crow. While shopping downtown, the lack of restrooms and dining facilities created difficulties, especially when she was out with her daughter. "We had to leave downtown," Brady said of those times. "She could not understand why we had to get in the car and drive all the way back to Central Avenue when she saw the lunch counters at Kress. We had to stop and explain. There was a lot of explaining."

As part of the NAACP Youth Corps, Gwendolyn Powell was among the young Black activists protesting segregation in the 1960s and challenging Tampa Theatre's racist admissions policy. Courtesy of Joyce Cotton.

After World War II, more Black citizens and returning veterans imagined a better future, a victory over fascism abroad and segregation back in the states. In 1954, the US Supreme Court's *Brown v. Board of Education* decision mandated the integration of the nation's public schools, but the pace of reform proved to be agonizingly slow. Impatient for a change toward equality, a new generation of Blacks extended their activism from the courtroom to the public square.

Brady bore witness to the change. "Martin Luther King came along and the whole world turned upside down," she said. The young woman soon became an activist, joining picket lines and sit-ins at segregated businesses. Mayor Nick Nuccio created a Biracial Committee composed mostly of business and activist leaders to help address the city's racial issues. His successor, Julian Lane, relied on the committee's leadership, headed by attorney Cody Fowler, to manage the city's desegregation.

In 1960, sit-ins by Black college students at lunch counters in Greensboro, North Carolina, inspired more demonstrations across the South. In many cities, chapters of the NAACP formed youth councils to harness the enthusiasm of young adults in nonviolent demonstrations. One of those youths was Gwendolyn Powell, who grew up in Tampa with a strong sense of self and a rebellious streak. "When nobody was watching," she recalled, "I drank water out of the white fountain. I didn't use the colored fountain. I never got caught either. I don't know what would have happened if I had." Her joining the NAACP Youth Council in the 1960s was a life-changing decision that placed her at the forefront of the local movement. Although in 1963 the federal Civil Rights Act seemed imminent in Congress, the motivated young activists continued to demonstrate against segregated businesses, including Tampa Theatre.

Powell recalled,

> We were organized and we were well dressed, and we had our manners. My friend and I, there would be two of us, and we'd go to the window, and we had a hundred-dollar bill. We would ask the lady for two tickets, "We'd like two tickets please, and you can keep the change." She said, "I'm sorry but I can't sell you tickets." So, we'd go away, somebody else would go and say, "Would you get us two tickets, please? You can keep the change." After a while, the lady was so nervous she had to leave. She was visibly shaking and somebody else came. We did that for a few days and it didn't last long because people were standing around, watching us like it was a parade. The downtown merchants didn't like it because people weren't shopping.

Faced with the pressure of regular protests, the owners of the theater did not know how to react. Based in Jacksonville, Florida State Theaters made itself unavailable when a local biracial committee tried to contact them about integrating. After several demonstrations, a company representative met with the group. In accordance with the Civil Rights Act of 1964, beginning that July, Tampa Theatre no longer excluded people of color.

After being barred from the Tampa Theatre for so long, Rowena Brady was unimpressed when she visited with her class as a teacher on a field trip years later. "I had no interest in going down there," she said. "They didn't want me before, I thought. Why should I go now? When I took my children, I said, 'You mean to tell me this is what they have been keeping me out of all these years? I don't believe it.' Like it was some king's palace."

Although her reaction to the theater was heavily influenced by her experiences during segregation, the theater in the early 1970s was not an impressive sight. Only one elderly usher remained, Oscar Licata, out of a squadron of fifteen. Much of the interior was covered with fifty years of dust and grime. With the blue sky peeling and most of the stars gone out, the atmospheric illusion no longer invited awe but ridicule.

Economic Decline and Blaxploitation

Tampa Theatre's fortunes declined sharply with the faltering central business district. The closing of Morrison's Cafeteria in 1968 was a bad omen. The beloved

By the late 1960s, the theater relied on B movies that catered to moviegoers' base impulses, such as *Mini Skirt Mob* (1968). Gandy Photo Collection, USF Digital Commons, used under CC-BY license.

cafeteria was a mainstay for a generation of residents, especially after church services. By then, even churchgoing had been relocated to the suburbs.

By the time Gary Ratliff was hired there as a maintenance man in 1969, Tampa Theatre was in disrepair. He recalled,

> The theater business downtown was very slow. Florida State Theaters had gotten so financially behind they started changing their program from mainstream Hollywood films to films that would appeal to the Black neighborhoods that are close to downtown here. They had more people walking up to the box office when they started showing those type of films. That's how they changed their business plan.

The Stewardesses drew crowds in 1971. Gary Ratliff recalled, "It was a 3D movie. People were standing in line all the way across the street waiting to get their little blue and red glasses to come in here and see it." *Tampa Tribune.*

"The old Tampa now has a different complexion." *Shaft* embodied the changing times and fortunes of the downtown relic. 1971. *Tampa Tribune.*

Just a few years after the theater integrated, Tampa Theatre and the Franklin across the street began screening blaxploitation films. These films featured strong Black characters in sensational and stylized productions. Inspired by Black directors, Black actors portrayed new heroes—Shaft, Dolemite, and Coffy—who exemplified aspects of Black identity. Judy Hamilton wrote in the *Tampa Daily Times* in 1973, "There is still some fun to be had in the Tampa Theatre today, but it is of a less genteel nature. The fun for the audience now often comes when a Black man on screen is doing violence to a White man, for the old Tampa now has a different complexion."

Film critic Steve Persall remembers his first encounter with blaxploitation as a teen at Tampa Theatre.

> The first time that I recall being here, aside from being a small child, was 1971. My dad and I came over to see *Shaft,* which at that time was making a lot of

ripples as the first Black action hero. We were probably the only two White people in the place. It was a matinee and not a big crowd, but the enthusiasm of that crowd, they were seeing something they had never seen before. I was able to sort of see it through their eyes and I was fourteen, fifteen years old, so I was pretty impressionable. That has stuck with me my whole life, that experience, that movie, and of course the location.

In the 1970s, the theater fell into disrepair. Gary Ratliff described the scene.

> Unfortunately a lot of customers were coming in the back door. You have forty kids coming in the other doors and seventy-year-old ushers working retirement jobs trying to keep them out. It was an impossible situation. The vandalism was rampant. It was not a pretty sight. One week I took every remaining light fixture off the wall. We locked everything up in the organ chambers, and we chained the balcony doors. The upstairs became storage.

Despite the difficulties, Tampa Theatre could still impress. Darryl Miles, who had been accustomed to attending movies in Black theaters, immediately took to the dream palace. "I remember thinking that the Tampa Theatre was much nicer than Lincoln," he said. "The seats were larger, the theater was larger, and I didn't know what mezzanines were, so I thought the theater had two balconies."

Gary Ratliff at the light board. He arrived to see the theater's last years as a private business and its transition to a community resource. Tampa Theatre.

Fallen Theaters

Like the downtown districts they occupied, movie palaces became anachronisms. The industry and environment that gave rise to movie palaces had changed dramatically since the heyday of the 1920s and suffered a succession of setbacks. The Great Depression was the first disaster that hampered business. Then radio programming came into its own in the 1930s, giving the public a free alternative to movies.

SOUTH FLORIDAS
MAAS BRO
1891

opposite Residents learned a bitter lesson in preservation when the iconic county courthouse was lost to the bulldozer over their objections in 1953. Robertson and Fresh Photograph Collection, USF Digital Commons.

The impact of television was staggering. In 1953, forty million people attended movies each week, fewer than half of the peak of ninety million in 1946–1948. Television forced Hollywood to increase the quality of movies, but quantity dropped, necessitating longer runs for films. Theater operators coped with declining attendance and longer runs by showing several features at a time in smaller spaces. The suburban multiplex, a cluster of several small theaters under one roof, was born in 1965. In the process, going to the movies had lost much of its sense of occasion.

The cities that once guaranteed the success of movie palaces now ensured their decline. By 1970, more people lived in the suburbs than in cities or the country. As suburbanites sprawled outward, they left impoverished inner cities, where rising crime discouraged movie attendance. Movie palaces became especially difficult to operate profitably as they aged and required more maintenance. Some of the old venues found new lives, while many fell to redevelopment. Too much of America's most exuberant architecture unceremoniously met the wrecking ball.

The decades after World War II found downtown Tampa in desperate straits. Much was lost in the name of dubious progress. The old Hillsborough County Courthouse designed by John A. Wood, a kind of architectural companion to the Tampa Bay Hotel, serves as a prime example. Despite the pleas of Tampa's preservation-minded residents, the minaret-crowned structure met the wrecking ball in 1953. That same year, Tampa's annexation of several suburbs such as Sulphur Springs and Palma Ceia doubled the area and population of the city overnight. As the city

top Drive-in theaters attracted viewers to outdoor screens in the suburbs. The Fun-Lan opened on Hillsborough Avenue in 1950. Courtesy of Tampa-Hillsborough County Public Library System.

bottom In 1958, the city held an ill-fated Snow Day in front of the theater. It did little to change downtown's sagging fortunes. Tampa Bay History Center.

Too many of the old movie palaces fell to the wrecking ball or worse. The Michigan Theater in Detroit once seated more than four thousand. Today, its shell is still used as a makeshift parking garage. 1976. Library of Congress.

sprawled into the hinterlands, its own built heritage seemed to be quickly disappearing, torn down in the name of progress or abandoned to blight and neglect. Shopping centers opened around the city, beginning with Britton and Northgate Plazas in the late 1950s, soon to be augmented by countless strip developments. In 1958, only about a quarter of the city's trade occurred downtown.

The 1960s and 1970s were especially dark days for Tampa's local landmarks. Urban renewal and interstate highways tore swaths through the urban fabric, displacing thousands of residents and dislocating communities. Ybor City and West Tampa were hit especially hard. In 1971, Falk's department store, at the same downtown address since 1898, went out of business. The remnants of the Black Central Avenue business district were removed in 1974. The Sulphur Springs arcade came down soon after that.

In reaction to the destruction of the nation's built heritage, Congress passed the National Preservation Act in 1966. It was hoped that citizens would be inspired to save the most distinctive parts of their communities. Many in Tampa answered that call in the 1970s when citizens formed the Tampa Historical Society and Tampa Preservation Inc. Both nonprofit groups established headquarters in Hyde Park houses long before the neighborhood was considered fashionable. The Ybor City State Museum opened to celebrate the old Latin Quarter's history just as it seemed to be slipping away. When restoration experts from the Historic American Building

City leaders spent twenty years trying to develop an open-air mall on Franklin Street, but the concept never caught on, circa 1970. Gandy Photo Collection, USF Digital Commons, used under CC-BY license.

Survey team visited in 1974, locals asked for their preservation advice. Consultant James A. Williams said, "You need to start with something big and the smaller things will fall in line."

A Passion for Preservation

Lee Duncan practically grew up with the movie industry. His stepfather ran three movie theaters in Tampa (the Casino, Royal, and Ritz), where Duncan worked in various positions growing up, from janitor to assistant manager. He met his future wife, Anna, at Hillsborough High School and found a partner for life. The Tampa Theatre was the epicenter of their courtship. After his shift at a different movie theater, "I'd get off work and pick her up," Duncan said, and they would proceed directly to the Colonnade on Bayshore back when it was still a drive-in specializing in burgers and olive-garnished Coke martinis.

> Then I'd have supper. I had enough money to buy a hamburger and two limeades, and she'd always want a bite of my hamburger. We would always sit in the same place [in the theater]. The ushers never worried about seating us because they knew where we were going to sit. As soon as you go inside the auditorium [in the balcony] you turn left, next to the wall, right by the mirror.

Lee and Anna Duncan on their wedding day in 1946. Courtesy of Anna Lee Duncan.

The couple graduated from the University of Tampa and married in January 1946. They went into the insurance business and operated the Airdrome Grill downtown. In 1951, a new challenge presented itself. "One day somebody asked me why I didn't run [for public office]. I thought about it and decided to do it," he explained. He soon began a tenure on the City Council that lasted thirty-six years.

Lee and Anna Duncan's daughter, Anna Lee, spoke fondly of her dad.

He was a wonderful father. Growing up he was just so sweet, so interested in people, and my parents doted on each other. The year I was born, my parents opened the family insurance business. I remember my mother saying, "I don't know what this man was thinking, I have a baby on the way." They started an insurance business and he went into politics. My mother, believe it or not, she loved politics. He was on the council of the Performing Arts Center. I think he did it to make my mother happy.

On Saturdays, my Sicilian grandmother would take us to the Tampa Theatre. We would ride the bus downtown and we just thought that was so exciting. We'd go into the Tampa Theatre, and I still remember to this day the spot that we sat in. It was a treat on Saturdays. Any time a new movie came out, that's what we would do. She would make her Italian hamburgers as she called them. I don't know how she made the sauce, but they were better than Goody Goodys. It was not a normal hamburger. Nana just thought that was better stuff to eat than the popcorn and everything. And she was saying, "You've got to make sure people don't see you eating your food," and that's what we would do. We looked forward to that every Saturday.

We used to love to go downtown. On Saturdays, we would get all dressed up, we'd go downtown, we'd shop, we'd have lunch, and then come back home. It was just one of those Saturday afternoon things. We'd go to Maas Brothers and other big department stores. Shoe shops, the five-and-dime, Kress. There was a Singer sewing center and my grandmother, who loved to sew, would love to go in there. We would always go to the Tampa Theatre and this was before my father had anything to do with it. I think that that was the only theater we knew growing up.

Later, he would talk about how he wanted to fight to save it. It's a beautiful place. I know he had conversations with a lot of different people as far as trying to pull everything together to be able to get it saved. It was something that he worked so hard on because he didn't want to see it demolished. He just glowed when he talked about it.

Lee Duncan was active in many organizations outside of City Council, but he may be remembered best for spearheading the effort to rescue Tampa Theatre. In 1991, the auditorium was dedicated to him in a ceremony with Mayor Sandy Freedman and bears his name today.

Rescue

In 1974, it no longer made any business sense for Florida ABC Theaters to continue operating the old palace. The venue did not generate profits and the tax burden was considerable. The owners signaled their desire to demolish the building. A profile of Tampa Theatre in the theater history journal *Marquee* frankly assessed the venue's many challenges at the time.

> The 1500 seat house was cursed with the smallest stage and tiniest proscenium on the southern Paramount circuit. The lovely atmospheric house is almost spoiled by the canted CinemaScope screen that was pushed out on the stage apron in front of their proscenium arch. The building has other limitations too. When the failing Paramount chain was dissolved during the depression, the Tampa lost control of its lobby to a separate owner of the office building over the street frontage. Consequently, such things as air conditioning for the lobby are supplied by the owner of the office building and utilities for the auditorium are completely separate. As if these complications weren't enough, the Tampa provides air conditioning for the theater across the street via underground ducts, and the recipient provides electrical current for the Tampa. Small wonder the Tampa survives. The legal technicalities alone would be enough to intimidate most redevelopers.

Despite the logistical challenges, there was a genuine love for the theater in the community, along with the resolve not to raze the city's history. It helped that most of the theater's supporters were probably unaware of just how complicated saving the structure would be. Tampa Theatre president John Bell recalled the efforts to preserve it.

> The potential loss of Tampa Theatre opened the eyes of a lot of people that there's some important buildings in Tampa that need some attention. The citizens began to call their City Council people. They began to call the mayor's office trying to figure out some way to save this building. We had great leadership from Lee Duncan, who was on the City Council at the time, and he took this under his wing. Joan Jennewein was very involved, the passion behind the scenes, feeding the civic leaders the information that was needed for them to make the case. There were many others.

The rescue effort began in 1974 with planning by Lee Duncan, Mayor Lloyd Copeland, and Raymond Mesler, executive director of the Tampa-Hillsborough Arts Council. They explored the idea of the city taking over the venue. There was a precedent for the city acquiring distinctive buildings. When railroad magnate Henry Plant died in 1899, his extravagant Tampa Bay Hotel was destined for bankruptcy. There were never enough wealthy vacationers to fill the massive Gilded Age palace. The city bought the hotel in 1904 for a fraction of its cost and leased it to operators who could never make it profitable. During the Great Depression, the hotel's ultimate failure presented city leaders with an acute dilemma in the early 1930s: sell the notable property, neglect it, or find a viable tenant. The newly founded University of Tampa presented an ideal solution by renting the property from the city for a dollar per year.

Hoping for a similar result for Tampa Theatre, Councilman Lee Duncan networked with the leadership of other preserved theaters around the country. He also conferred with Lamar Sera, ABC Florida Theaters' attorney, about a possible donation to the city. Duncan recalled the conversation: "I said, 'Your company made nothing but money, why can't you donate to the city of Tampa? It's a good write-off—it's for the city.'"

Tampa Mayor William F. Poe was not "an arts guy," but he understood the importance of saving something from downtown's crumbling past. 2001. Jeff Fay.

In April 1975, the City Council began to formally seek the donation of the theater. The preservation of the palace was seen as a vital and visible first step in reviving downtown Tampa. Mayor Bill Poe hoped it could be a catalyst for investments by businesses in downtown redevelopment projects. Mrs. H. L. Culbreath and other influential locals strongly supported the effort. "Surely," Culbreath wrote in a letter, "the palace could be kept open rather than having this beautiful interior ruined beyond repair. The Tampa Theatre was so much a part of Tampa and all of our lives. I'm sure there will be support for this project." In 1975, a feasibility study funded by a variety of public and private groups recommended that the City of Tampa accept title to the theater.

Councilman Lee Duncan spent two years carefully aligning support for the rescue. In January 1976, four City Council members shocked him by voting against the donation, and it failed.

> I thought everything was working smooth. I brought it before City Council to accept the theater for a dollar. We got everyone to agree on everything completely. Then we have four votes against it. The Arts Council made a statement that you could never get the smell of popcorn and collard greens out of it. Do you know who eats collard greens? Us Crackers and Black people.

The dissenting City Council members were justifiably wary of renovation costs and unsure the theater could ever turn a profit. The city was also in the process of building a new multimillion-dollar cultural complex. The Arts Council was afraid that accepting the theater would threaten its plans for a performing arts center. The editors of the *Tampa Tribune* advised the city to pass on the deal.

The commissioners who voted against the theater's acquisition had valid reasons for doing so. Commissioner Jan Platt thought the costs were too high. Sandy Freedman did not think enough people would visit downtown to keep the venue afloat. Lloyd Copeland thought that maintenance would be more costly than outlined in the budget and doubted its preservation would make any difference in the long-term recovery of downtown. Mayor Poe condemned the naysayers as being "short-sighted."

After a visit to the theater, *Tampa Times* journalist Robert Martin reflected,

> To walk into such an environment is to suddenly enter a world apart as one lets his senses and mind respond to it all, forgetting the tensions and problems outside those glass doors. Whether or not Tampa Theatre is worth saving as an historical structure I do not know. And, of course, if we continue tearing down all of our buildings before they reach their old age, we'll never have the option of deciding. But I do know that the interior of this old movie house is unusual in Tampa, and that another will never be built like it, and that it gives me pleasure to be able to walk into it and think about what it must have been like back in the good old days.

Councilman Duncan shored up additional support and again brought the issue before his colleagues. On April 30, 1976, the City Council approved the purchase of Tampa Theatre from ABC Florida State Theaters of the Smyrna-Halifax Corporation for one dollar.

John Bell recounted,

By a four-to-three City Council vote, Tampa Theatre still stands today. Mayor Poe understood that it was an important thing to save. He told me once, "I'm not an arts guy and I don't know that I'll be attending Tampa Theatre very much." But he said, "I realized that downtown was in such decline in the early seventies that we had to send a signal to the business community that the city was not going to abandon downtown Tampa. Tampa Theatre was the place where we could plant our flag. That's why I wanted to save it."

Since that time, within the two blocks surrounding us there's been more than $400 million of private sector investment, and residential towers, office buildings, hotels, restaurants, all kinds of retail. Every single one of those tout their proximity to the Tampa Theatre as a selling point. That tells me that it did have that type of catalytic effect. Tampa Theatre certainly lived up to what Mayor Poe hoped it would do, which was to attract attention and investment back in downtown.

It was put on the National Register of Historic Places in 1978. In 1988, Plant Hall at the University of Tampa and Tampa Theatre were the first inductees as city landmarks. You can tell a lot about a community's values simply through those places which it chooses to preserve. When they choose a place as beautiful and as special and as meaningful as Tampa Theatre, it says a lot about the soul of this community.

Survival

The city allocated $150,000 for restoration efforts, and the process began with a good scrubbing. Although the city had publicized a gentle, mild cleaning using compressed air, Gary Ratliff recalled the use of pressure hoses in the proscenium. "Whatever dust and dirt there was just dripped down to the side and on the floor. The orchestra pit was deep in black goop by the time they got through. Mud puddles. I started cleaning it." The city installed new red seats, refurbished the ceiling, positioned the antiques, and restored Eberson's trademark, a stuffed peacock.

One of the city's civil engineers, Bill Garrett, was highly impressed during his inspections of the structure. "This theater was constructed with some of the finest engineering I have ever laid eyes on," he said. "Built like a fortress [it] boggles the mind. When I first looked at this thing, I had reservations, but the more I looked, the more impressed I got." He obtained blueprints, but no schematics of the byzantine

The City of Tampa gave the theater a restorative makeover before reopening that included a thorough cleaning, new seats, a new stage, and much more. 1976. Tampa Theatre.

electrical system could be found, so any renovation of the electrical system would have to be done "wire by wire."

The list of improvements made by the city after the rescue is impressive. The initial restoration, which depended heavily on volunteers, lasted eight months. The *Tampa Tribune* reported that the effort included "the replacement of old seating and a worn carpet, extensive stage repair, rehabilitation of the orchestra pit, comprehensive repainting and plasterwork, and the careful restoration of some 450 original theater artifacts." The city's public works department was given orders to "install a new mechanical plant, augment acoustical quality with modern sound equipment, fortify the electrical system, adjust lighting, and maintain service facilities."

After its reopening, the city hired Jack Casey to restore the theater's interior paint. Casey poured his soul into the job, and with his assistant John Gurbacs repainted the proscenium. Anyone familiar with John Eberson's exquisite use of paint would have been daunted. As Casey described it, the incredibly tedious work included matching pigments to the original colors, then laying down an umber base coat, followed by an umber wash and eleven individual shades of color. Local sculptor Dan Rahenkamp took the theater's statues back to his studio, where they were repaired or recast. Other vital improvements included handicap access and hot water. These improvements were encouraging, but the Arts Council estimated it would take a half-million dollars to complete the restoration.

Reopening

Harrison Giddens grew up in Alabama and moved to Tampa as a young woman. After returning from her studies at Baylor University, she was eager to join Tampa's social scene. Giddens recalled,

> I got to know some of the folks that were moving and shaking. Lee Duncan was hell-bent to keep this place, get this place back to where people came and saw shows. I was asked to be one of the three women that helped reopen it. I served with Martha Ferman and Joan Jennewein. Looking back on it, they were ready to have some young people do the heavy lifting. It was a very special time because there wasn't a whole lot of renovation done before that. I remember opening night very clearly and I always wanted to be on stage, and I got to that night, the three of us. I would say that Miss Ferman and Joan

below The theater's grand reopening in January 1977 drew a who's who of Tampa society. Joan Jennewein, Lee Duncan, Harrison Giddens, and an unidentified man (*left to right*) attended the event. Tampa Theatre.

above and right In its premiere as a community theater, the reopening party packed the house. 1977. Tampa Theatre.

> Jennewein were probably in their early sixties. Now I'm older than they were. The three of us worked as a team and it was more about the opening. Can we fill it up? Can we get enough people here? How much of a party can we have?

The theater even brought back its first organist, Eddie Weaver, to play like he did in the old days. He had been winding down his career playing at the Byrd Theatre in Richmond, Virginia. Weaver promised a set list of classics, adding, "I would love seeing the old theater again and thinking back with a lot of the folks. Boy, those were the days."

For the theater's fifty-fifth birthday in 1981, members of the Gulf Coast Symphony accompanied *The Mark of Zorro* (1920). Tampa Theatre.

On January 22, 1977, the city staged a grand reopening of the theater for 1,500 patrons who paid twenty-five dollars per ticket. Prominent citizens publicly reserved seats. Harrison Giddens described the occasion.

> That night, all of old Tampa came. It was a blur; everybody came in their finest bib and tucker. Women still wore furs. It was cold. A radio station did a couple of interviews, where people could call in and tell their memories. One of the women called in and said, "What about the water fountains? They were filled with rose petals every time you came to the theater." That just came to us out of the blue. That night they were filled with rose petals. I remember we sat in the balcony but I don't remember the show. I just remember being a part of it.

The Frank Rey dancers staged a ballet inspired by the 1920s, and several film shorts were shown, including a sing-along. The main feature was Douglas Fairbanks in the *The Black Pirate,* accompanied by Weaver's playing. With the Wurlitzer still in disarray, he played an electric organ. The event concluded with the singing of "God Bless America."

It Almost Seems Alive

Attracting a consistent audience to the remnants of downtown would be no easy feat. For the next stage of its life, Tampa Theatre would be operated by the Tampa-Hillsborough Arts Council. The council gave the theater a simple mission: "to provide space for the visual arts (primarily cinema, limited drama and exhibits), enhance the image and attractiveness of downtown by generating human activity, [and] benefit the amateur artist or performer." A clause in the sale agreement prohibited the theater from showing 35mm films, which precluded its functioning as a modern cinema. As exquisite as Tampa Theatre was, it lacked a stage for major live productions. It would have to get by on vintage 16mm films and smaller live events. The theater began hosting field trips from local schools, introducing several generations of young residents to its charms.

Bob Holtzman ran the theater for more than a year just after its rescue. With little experience, Holtzman struggled initially but soon found his stride. In 1977, the theater drew fewer than 40,000, then attendance rose sharply the following year. Holtzman helped to build a popular film club that offered classic movies all year for a single fee, giving members the option to vote for films to be added to the series. He scheduled well-attended concerts that drew in new patrons. Holtzman was irritated when the Arts Council demanded a report on the problems of the venue. He wrote in the report, "For either the city fathers, the Arts Council or anybody else to expect the Tampa Theatre to have been a rip-snorting success from the start is avoiding the realities." The stark truth was that the underfunded theater was somehow expected to thrive in an ugly, blighted, crime-ridden downtown while the city invested millions in a new arts complex.

As the first director under the city, Bob Holtzman's tenure successfully relaunched Tampa Theatre, with strengths in classic cinema and live music. 1977. © Tampa Bay Times/Zuma Press.

The *Tampa Tribune* editorialized in 1978, "It has been an interesting fourteen months since opening. Now the film club has two thousand subscribers [and] events staged during the weekday nights and weekends are almost always filled. Security complaints have stopped. That's a solid triumph over the demolition crews—and something of which Tampa can be proud." This was high praise from a newspaper that opposed the rescue of Tampa Theatre in the first place.

Tampa Theatre could rock with the best of them. Here Dee Ramone of the Ramones rumbles on bass. 1981. Dimetri Maderakis.

The film club was one of one of the theater's early public programming successes. Concentrating on vintage films made the best use of the antiquated 16mm projector. 1977. *Tampa Tribune.*

Live music became a more consistent part of programming after the theater's rescue. There was no better place for jazz in 1978. *St. Petersburg Times.*

The city gave the theater a mandate to serve the community. Here, the city's Recreation Department held a talent show that would have been impossible twenty years before. City of Tampa Archives.

To replace Holtzman when he relocated to Miami, the Arts Council hired Vernita Batchelder, who held a PhD in theater. Several months after her arrival she noted,

> Bob had done a wonderful job of recreating interest in the theater and beginning to get people to come back downtown. When I look at some of the problems we are faced with, it really helps to be able to laugh out loud. We don't have adequate facilities for productions of any size. I'd really like to offer more to senior citizens. Our 99 cents Jazz Jam has been a success and we'd like to expand, maybe offering bluegrass one week and jazz the next.
>
> This theater is the kind of place that almost seems alive, and I guess I feel like I have to protect and nurture it in a way. When I first started, I would walk through the halls upstairs and downstairs by myself. It's kind of eerie, but this place has so much charm. It's the kind of building you won't see again.

The theater was a new burden for the city during a difficult time. Between the lease and routine maintenance costs, the theater cost taxpayers $100,000 annually to keep open, with personnel and programming budgets costing about $80,000 more. The emphasis on classic cinema garnered a ready audience, and the theater prospered in the early 1980s. The film club attracted three thousand members by 1982. The following year, it operated with a surplus of $160,000, a remarkable feat for a theater with little more than a 16mm projector. Earl Screiber, director of the Tampa-Hillsborough Arts Council, said, "The Tampa Theatre has been enormously successful. It reopened five years ago in a downtown that died every day at 5:05 p.m."

Batchelder complained of the conditions downtown and paltry funding.

> At least Tampa Theatre seems to be an anchor for the downtown area. We need to get to the point where there are more restaurants staying open late, more nightlife. Given the staff and the equipment and the money we have to operate with, I think we're doing a damn good job. We've got programs that

Founders Life

Franklin Street, circa 1980. Gandy Photo Collection, USF Digital Commons, used under CC-BY license.

> pay for themselves. Our biggest problem has been letting people know that we're here and telling them what's available. There are people in Tampa who don't even know we exist. I can't really complain about our relationship with the city and the Arts Council. The city considers it a kind of public service by funding it as it does.

Batchelder called for greater funding, more publicity, and more promoters to book events.

When needled about budget woes, Batchelder said she felt lucky to draw any patrons to a desolate downtown where many felt unsafe. A journalist observed, "The theater's marquee lights on Franklin Street are just about the only signs of life downtown after dark since thirty years ago at least."

opposite Tampa and Ashley Streets, circa 1980. At its lowest point in the 1970s and 1980s, downtown Tampa was all but abandoned after 5 p.m. Gandy Photo Collection, USF Digital Commons, used under CC-BY license.

EXIT

New president John Bell was alarmed by one aspect of the theater: its nonexistent backstage. Tampa Theatre.

4

Love at First Sight

When John Bell first arrived as Tampa Theatre's new president in 1985, he recognized the position as a great opportunity. The challenges he would face only became apparent after his arrival.

> I got the theater bug in high school and decided to major in theater in college. I knew early on, although I enjoyed acting and directing and those things, I never wanted to live the life of an actor because there's a lot of rejection involved. I was intrigued with the notion of arts administration, the management side of the arts business. So that's what I focused on, and I was fortunate to get my first job out of college at the North Carolina Arts Council.
>
> My dad was a Methodist minister, which meant that we moved like clockwork to a new town and a new church. Growing up, my playground was the empty sanctuary during the week. After working in historic theaters, I began to realize that there was this similarity between the buildings. An empty theater felt to me much like an empty sanctuary. I think that has to do not necessarily with the architecture but with the sense of humanity that's in both of those types of buildings and the sort of spirituality that coincides with that.
>
> After I left the North Carolina Arts Council, I took over the management of a historic theater that had just been saved in Greensboro, North Carolina. It was the Carolina Theater, built in 1927, the same era as Tampa Theatre. I got that job when I was twenty-five. I had some success there, stayed for six years, and became more aware of the other historic theaters that had been saved around the country. This opportunity came up in 1985, and I had been aware of Tampa Theatre. I knew it was a significant building built by an important architect and it was a bigger market. I threw my hat in the ring and was fortunate enough to get the job.
>
> During my final interview, I was brought in by Art Keeble, who was the director of the Arts Council, which was governing the theater at the time. I

John Bell on his first day working at Tampa Theatre, 1985. He was happy when he found how much work remained to be done. Tampa Theatre.

remember walking in and just stopping and it took my breath away. I remember gasping. I had been in many historic theaters before but there was something really special about walking into that foyer and to this auditorium. It was love at first sight for me.

Bell described programming at Tampa Theatre at the time.

When I arrived in 1985, the theater was in okay condition. It was doing some concert events, and it was doing its one-off repertory [classic] film program, but that was already in decline. I will give prior management credit in that they had done a good job of getting it up and running. I had moved to a theater that was on its surface doing really well. Attendance was pretty good.

He observed the limitations and advantages of the space.

This theater cannot handle most of the performing arts because of the tiny stage. They covered what used to be the orchestra pit with a stage, and that gave the theater the ability to host comedians, music groups, touring attractions, and some small live events. It was never really considered like a true performing arts venue. It was always this hybrid. That was kind of a shock for me when I got here, even though I'd seen the stage, I didn't realize how limiting that could be in some respects. I just looked at the staff and said, "Well, let's not worry about what we can't do. Let's not think about expanding the stage. What are we good at?"

We're considered an attractive intimate space in which to experience a concert. If you're an audience member, in the very top of the balcony, you're still only eighty feet from the stage. And if you're in the front row of the mezzanine, you're twenty-five feet from the stage. So, it's very close because you're in the same room with the artist. You're not separated by the moat of an orchestra pit. In spite of the fact that it's twelve hundred seats, it has this very cozy feel to it.

One of the more troubling times for the theater after I arrived was actually in the first couple of years. The film industry was changing in the mid-eighties. Back then if you wanted to see an old movie without any dog food commercials, you had to come to a theater like Tampa Theatre that was showing repertory films. That was changing because cable was beginning to enter the marketplace. We had things called VCRs [video cassette recorders], where you could go to a store and rent one and watch it at home. All of that began to erode the need for people to come to a theater to see an old movie.

What I didn't fully appreciate when I first started was that the decline in that prior programming model had already begun. Then as I looked at charts from the early eighties and then after my first or second year I realized, "Oh, the revenues are going down." How do we right this ship in the face of all of these headwinds that we've got in the marketplace?

The Wurlitzer Awakening

The theater's artist-in-residence organist Steven Ball explained some history of the theater organ.

> When theaters were under such stress economically, if the instrument [organ] didn't make the revenue it needed to justify its existence, they were mothballed. The organs found a use by playing preshow music, music for the intermissions, ambient music. That concept of an organ concert in a theater was invented by George Wright, who took some of these organs out of mothballs in the 1950s. It was a culture built around the concept of an amateur, an enthusiast of the organ, who joined a theater organ club. It was those clubs which rescued many of these organs from theaters. A culture formed around these instruments. From all those thousands of instruments, there are currently about forty in their original homes. This is one of them, although the way it currently appears is not its original configuration.

Volunteers from the Central Florida Theater Organ Society helped recover and reassemble parts of the Mighty Wurlitzer, Tampa Theatre's heart, circa 1985. Tampa Theatre.

Perhaps the most difficult task in the theater's comeback was buying and restoring an organ to replace the original. When organist Eddie Ford left, the instrument fell silent. In

Organist extraordinaire Lee Erwin (*left*) was decisive in completing the organ rebuild and as an accompanist. He is pictured here with John Bell in 1996. Tampa Theatre.

1954, management sold the organ pipes to Lane Coachman, who donated them to Bayshore Baptist Church in Tampa. The console went to an out of state buyer. Led by president Ewell Stanford, the Central Florida Theater Organ Society developed a plan to bring back the original pipes and install parts of another organ to create a superior new instrument. Stanford had a special connection with theater organs. At age eighteen, he had been hired by Publix Theatres to tour the South as its house organist. He returned to Tampa many years later to open an organ store on Kennedy Boulevard.

In about 1979, Bayshore Baptist Church sold the instrument to the Central Florida Theater Organ Society for $4,500 but retained its console and four ranks of pipes. They acquired a console formerly used by WMCU radio in New York. A group of about twelve members of the organ society worked weekends to assemble the instrument, investing several thousand hours of donated labor. Every pipe had to be stripped, sanded and releathered using sheepskin. Steven Ball recounted, "It was a slow process. We had our local theater organ club, who were enthusiastic about it, but they didn't have a lot of know-how. They took this instrument piecemeal out of storage, put it all in the theater, and it evidently sounded quite terrible." The project took more time and money than expected, prompting benefit events such as a 1981 concert by Larry Ferrari, who played an electric organ to raise the money to complete the rebuilding of the wind chest. In 1982, the city acquired another set of pipes to complete the instrument. When restored, the pipe organ became one of only six working in Florida.

Restoring the Wurlitzer allowed Tampa Theatre to do what it was born to do: authentic "live" silent film. 1994. *Tampa Tribune*.

The theater's rebuilt organ made a triumphant return in 1985 when Hilton Jones accompanied the silent film *The Thief of Baghdad* (1924). Musicians from the Florida Orchestra played along, and characters costumed as Marilyn Monroe and the Marx Brothers roamed the theater between screenings. Even the ushers were clad in fanciful mock-Arabian garb. The future of silent features was assured that same year when the Arts Council hired new leadership in John Bell. He recalled,

> The organ society volunteers took years to complete the process. I think they were still working on it when I got here. When they fired it up, I thought, this doesn't sound like a theater organ. It was muddy, and it was then I discovered

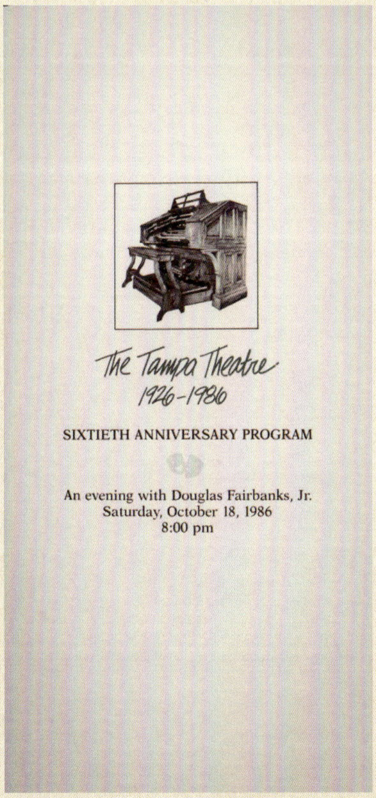

The Black Pirate (1926) is the earliest surviving film shown at Tampa Theatre, screened on its third day of operations, October 17, 1926. A pirate story shot in color, it remains part of the theater's silent film presentations today. For the theater's sixtieth anniversary, in 1986, guests went back to where it all began, *The Black Pirate* with a functional Wurlitzer and a guest appearance by Douglas Fairbanks Jr.

top left Original poster, 1926. *Tampa Tribune.*

bottom left John Bell with Douglas Fairbanks Jr., 1986. *Tampa Tribune.*

top right Ticket to the event, 1986. Tampa Theatre.

bottom right Invitation to the anniversary event, 1986. Tampa Theatre.

> that they put it in backwards. By backwards, I mean you're supposed to have the small flutes and piccolos in the front, and the big boys in the back. For all the criticism that I had, I did keep in the back of my mind that this group of people had the foresight to get that organ and bring it back.

The arrival of John Bell as the theater's new president was decisive. For Bell, being able to properly show silent films with Wurlitzer accompaniment was a core function of the facility and a selling point that could not be ignored. He called on theater organ expert Lee Erwin to help the stalled rebuilding effort. Steven Ball observed, "Lee was one of the original players back in the day, and he knew what a theater organ should sound like. It was John Bell, his vision, and his connection to Lee, which is what saved all of this. He helped get them on the right track and started presenting silent movies here again."

The recalibrated Wurlitzer premiered in 1986 when the theater screened *The Black Pirate,* which was attended by Douglas Fairbanks Jr. to offer some commentary on his father's role in the classic.

Wings of Desire

When she was first elected in 1987, Linda Saul-Sena became the only woman on Tampa City Council. "All six men [on the council] wanted to be on the Sports Authority, and they fought over it, and that kind of determined who became chairman. I was the only one who wanted to be on the Arts Council," she said. While she loved Tampa Theatre, she was shocked at the state of affairs behind the curtain. She spoke of her tenure on the Tampa-Hillsborough Arts Council.

> I was chair for a couple of years. I'd meet on a maybe monthly basis with John at his office there. If you know the beginning of the *Maltese Falcon,* where you feel like Sam Spade's office is really old, that's what it felt like. It had the energy of a bootstrap operation. You think of films being Hollywood and glamorous, slick and shiny. This was grassroots and scrappy.

After Bell's arrival as director in 1985, the theater's financial performance became a concern. With much of the appetite for classic movies satisfied by cable television, programmers could no longer rely on that old staple. An early demand for art films, also known as specialty films, collapsed with the age of the VCR.

Linda Saul-Sena and her husband, Mark, attend Oscar Night 2008. Tampa Theatre.

Bell also had to reckon with persistent problems involving the audio quality. Writing of a discussion with friends after a movie at Tampa Theatre, a local film critic observed, "Half of their conversation was devoted to complaining about not being able to hear the movie. Poor sound quality at Tampa's sole art house is sometimes a reality." Looking back, Bell reasoned, "The equipment installed in 1978 wasn't bad, but many prints sounded muddy and unintelligible. The problem was that engineers had underestimated the complexity of the acoustics in the auditorium." State Representative Helen Gordon Davis was able to earmark $50,000 of state funds for a new sound system as part of the 1988 Cultural Facilities Program. Audio wizard Hank Lamb custom-built a modern surround-sound system and used a special coating on parts of the ceiling to minimize the theater's echo.

Ultimately, Bell knew the theater needed to make some big changes to stay viable.

With the support of new technology, Tampa Theatre becomes a first-run house again for the first time in more than a decade. 1988. *Tampa Tribune.*

"The answer was to get back to first-run films to give us the ability to be more relevant to people," he explained. "It's not that we would totally abandon showing older films, but the new films were the way for us to get going again." That would require an upgrade from the theater's old 16mm projector to an expensive 35mm model. Mark Sena, husband of City Councilwoman Linda Saul-Sena, had long been a champion of Tampa Theatre. In 1988, he became a legend. "The real issue," Sena said, "was that they needed better equipment, but they didn't have the money to buy it." As senior vice president of communications at Equity Associates, Sena mentioned the theater's distress to a client. Stuart Blair, chairman of UA Communications Inc. in Denver, a corporation of movie theaters, was sympathetic. Blair offered two 35mm projectors worth $40,000.

When Bell learned the projectors were available for pickup in Jacksonville, he jumped at the chance and drove there immediately. He said of the donated equipment at the time, "It's maybe seven years old. To them, it's obsolete. To us, it's state-of-the-art." It was a transformational moment for the theater, when it could throw off the shackles of its noncompetitive agreement with ABC Theaters (which had gone out of business) and join the modern cinema market. It seems appropriate that the first film to be screened with the new hardware was *Wings of Desire,* an instant cult classic about angels and romance.

The new equipment and first-run films couldn't have come at a more opportune time. In 1988, the theater had a $40,000 deficit, which alarmed the Arts Council. "There were some interesting board meetings when we were losing all that money," Bell said. "Being able to turn it around certainly was a very important thing, not only for the theater, but for me. We made that switch and immediately began to turn around our fortunes." In 1990, the theater set records for attendance and concession sales.

Director of programming Diane Eberly said she welcomed the change that the new projector allowed.

> I found it to be far more interesting than doing old movies, though I love old movies. I'm thrilled to know that when we aren't the only house playing a film, we often outgross the commercial houses. We play a lot fewer shows, and we

After the rescue, the city changed the auditorium's color scheme, favoring red for the seats, curtains, and accents. Eberson would have disapproved. He thought red was an undesirable color for theaters. 1989. Tampa Theatre.

John Bell (*front, second from the left*) with the theater crew, circa 1990. Tampa Theatre.

charge less. We also have over 1,400 seats. These other places put their art films in their 150 seaters. We lucked into having the projector donated to us at that point in time.

Bell was determined that future upgrades would not be relegated to luck. He knew that most improvements could only proceed with more funding. The slow pace of renovation dictated by razor-thin budgets could only result in long-term neglect. "Tampa Theatre really lacked community involvement," he reasoned. "Organizations which have direct ties to private-sector support are always stronger and more dynamic in the long run than those which rely only on government support." Accordingly, in 1992, Bell convinced the Arts Council to allow Tampa Theatre to form its own nonprofit support organization, Tampa Theatre Inc., which made fundraising more practical. He also formed a five-member board of directors that gradually grew in membership and responsibilities over the years. Bell explained,

> I began to realize that the Arts Council, as it was constituted, could not possibly get us where we needed to go because we needed a huge infusion of money, both for programming and for long-term restoration. The council is not a fundraising organization. It was applying for state grants, and we could not apply because we were from the same agency. That's why we formed the nonprofit Tampa Theatre Inc., to be able to access those grants, create a membership program, and start growing that way on the contributed revenue side. We didn't have a dedicated board. It was clear to me that we needed more resources and more people involved and focused on the theater.
>
> Just as the two facilities [Tampa Theatre and the Straz Center for the Performing Arts] can coexist with complementary programming, we've discovered that we can coexist in fundraising as well. We have each had successful fundraising campaigns, sometimes simultaneously. The bottom line

is that today Tampa can boast two nationally recognized cultural facilities in the Straz and the Tampa Theatre. We complement each other very well.

While Bell was on a campaign to win new friends for the theater, he also showed he could be firm when crossed. When termites had been found in the building, including the office tower above, theater staff won a grant to fumigate the entire facility. After two years of trying to coordinate a window of several days when everyone could vacate the building, he ran out of patience with a large law firm with offices upstairs. Finally, the firm offered to vacate on Thanksgiving weekend, a time when the fumigation company was closed for the holiday. It became so contentious that Bell faxed a news release to the press reading, "Termites and lawyers, aren't they the same thing?" Finally, the firm agreed to vacate for a couple days so the procedure could take place.

Summer Classics

Just as the theater was making headway with contemporary films using its new projector, classics made a comeback repackaged as summer programming. Aside from offering vintage movies in a timeless setting, many of the events included post-screening discussions of the films and their histories with film critics and other experts. Customers also enjoyed a chance to escape Florida's heat and humidity.

The Summer Classic series has been a pillar of programming since the early 1990s. 2009. *Tampa Tribune.*

Bell recalled,

> In the early nineties, I took a chance. All of my colleagues that were running similar film programs around the country were telling me that there was no future in showing classic films. I thought they were wrong. It took a couple of years before it caught on. Now it's one of our most popular series. I think it's the longest-running classics film series in the state of Florida now. Any Sunday afternoon between June and August, you come to the Tampa Theatre around three o'clock, and you'll find at least seven hundred people. It's not uncommon for us to sell out a film that's fifty or sixty years old.

Communications director Tara Schroeder described the social aspect of attending films there: "People get here really early and talk to each other as they stand in line, then they linger in our lobby and mingle, and then finally they go in the auditorium and listen to the organ before the film begins."

Dianne Persall, a frequent attendee with her husband, film critic Steve Persall, had this recollection:

> Almost any of the classic movie series, half the audience, it's their first time seeing it. It's so fun to be there with them. And you can tell when people haven't seen it before because they're reacting. Then you have people who know and love the movie. They are so excited, and it's so fun to be there. Depending on the movie sometimes you will have a talk back or response.

A restored 3D version of *Creature from the Black Lagoon* has reacquainted audiences with the classic. 2009. Tampa Theatre.

Bell described similar effects.

> People love coming into this building and having that experience, almost like time travel, of watching a film like *Casablanca* on the screen with twelve hundred people they

don't know, in the dark. Everyone's seen the movie, but you're all having that communal experience together. If it were in any other building, it probably wouldn't work. You hit this critical mass of people, five hundred, six hundred, seven hundred. Even though six hundred people is only 50 percent capacity for us, when you get six hundred people in here, it feels full. It feels really successful and then there's this buzz that happens, there's an electricity. When you get a big crowd like that, then it's a magical thing.

Activist and photographer Bobby Smith documented the closeted Tampa of the 1950s. This photo of an unknown bodybuilder onstage was in his collection. Bobby Smith Photograph Collection, USF Digital Commons.

Come Out, Come Out, Wherever You Are

Many of the events held at Tampa Theatre were unthinkable in its life as a private business in a conservative Southern town. There was little room for art films or foreign cinema back then. After its rescue by the city, the events held there greatly widened in scope. For example, the Ebony Fashion Fair held its annual show at Tampa Theatre for many years. When that local tradition began in the 1950s, having the event at a White-only venue would have been impossible. In 1999, the palace hosted both the Gulf Coast Jewish Film Festival and Tampa Bay Jewish Film Festival. The same could be said for the Tampa International Gay and Lesbian Film Festival, which began and thrived at Tampa Theatre.

During the mid- to late 1980s, Mark Puig was a closeted gay man successful in the banking world. After becoming more involved politically, he began a new journey out of the closet, embracing a far more public role in the LGBTQ community, he said.

> During the late eighties, I was not out. I was vice president of operations at a bank, and I was definitely not out in the office. I did attend Metropolitan Community Church, a gay church. Tampa City Council was considering adding sexual orientation as a protected class in the human rights ordinance. My minister asked people to attend [a city council meeting], and I did. Sitting

there, after hours of antigay vibes, I finally got up [to speak] and my minister says, "Do you know what you're doing?" And I said, "Yes."

I testified, and right after I spoke, several members of the media approached me to do an interview and to take my picture. The next morning on the front page of the *St. Pete Times* was my picture and the interview. I went to work and said, "Okay, this is my last day." My co-worker looked at me and said, "John wants to see you in the office right now." In my mind I wondered, "How many boxes am I going to need? When is security coming up?" I went to see him, and he was a real good old boy. He said, "You know, I don't approve of your lifestyle." I said, "I can understand that." He said, "But you're one of the best managers I've ever had, and your job is secure."

It was then that I realized no matter how many laws are passed and court decisions are made in favor of the community, progress only happens when hearts are changed and people get to know someone who is LGBTQ. I decided right then and there to be a full-time gay activist in Tampa. I quit the bank and created a company called Tampa Bay Arts Incorporated, which is a nonprofit, and under that umbrella we had the Tampa Bay Gay Men's Chorus. At the same time, gay and lesbian film festivals were popping up all over the country in the major cities. So [in 1989] we decided, why don't we have a fundraiser and show a film at Tampa Theatre? Of course, I was real nervous, I thought, "We'll never do it."

When the theater reopened, I was just in high school. It was jaw-dropping. "Oh my god, this theater was going to be bulldozed." From then on out, I attended the screenings regularly. That's why I thought, "Let me talk to John [Bell] and see what he thinks about screening a gay film." We looked through a rental contract. We were a nonprofit, and there was no reason why we shouldn't be able to present a film. But there was a lot of flak and the Arts Council got involved. They approved it with a proviso that we could only show G, PG, and R-rated films.

After the film event for Pride Week in 1989, Puig and Keith Roberts kicked off the area's first gay film festival the following year. Publicity materials included the call, "Come out, come out, wherever you are." The festival in 1990 showed five films, a collaboration between the Tampa Bay Business Guild, the Tampa Bay Human Rights Organization, and the Tampa Bay Gay Men's Chorus. K. J. Mohr, who later

Tampa Theatre has hosted the Tampa International Gay and Lesbian Film Festival since the event's founding in 1990. 2015. Courtesy of Renee Cossette and Nick Cardello Photography.

served as the festival's director of programming, observed how controversial it was at the time: "Folks were closeted and scared because it was a radical act to be out and to come to an LGBT film festival." Still, it was an idea whose time had come. Like Puig at his old banking job, the gay community had been suppressed for too long. What became the Tampa International Gay and Lesbian Film Festival quickly found a passionate audience.

Puig described that first film festival.

> It was extremely exciting. The festival is one of the few places that LGBTQ people could go to be seen and to see movies with the characters that represented their identity. We had really huge audiences that first weekend. Next year, we expanded to three nights, Friday, Saturday, Sunday. Huge audiences.

Then we made the big decision to go ten days from a Friday to the following Sunday, with multiple screenings each night and several screenings on the weekend days. Once again, really high attendance. In fact, when we had the world premiere of *Priscilla, Queen of the Desert* [1994], we sold out the theater and there were lines wrapped around it. After the first or second year, we thought about changing those dates to October because National Coming Out Day had just been established on October 12. That was a very smart move.

In 1992, we submitted applications to receive a grant from the Hillsborough Arts Council. We were awarded those grants and it made the media, let me tell you. Front page news. Huge public outcry. So much, in fact, that they had to schedule a hearing to determine whether or not that grant should be rescinded. I had to testify in so many hearings. We actually had the support of hotels and venues. A majority of the City Council members voted to affirm the grant, which meant that our literature had the Tampa Arts logo. When it first opened, the crowd was not with us, let's just say that.

Festival director Renee Cosette said,

When we started here it was very hostile times. The Klan used to come and protest in full regalia. We had kids in their little Klan outfits. As time went by, they kind of disappeared, but I had this one persistent protester. Every year he would come, and it became a game. I'd apply for permits to close Franklin Street. He would pull our permit and know exactly what he was allowed and not allowed to do. He started going over to TECO [Tampa Electric Company] Plaza because that was public. He would stand across the street and use his bullhorn. It was horrible. It was owned by TECO and they wouldn't take a stand. So I had to rent the plaza. I rented the stairs so he couldn't go up there either.

We would hire off-duty police officers, and it was always the LGBT police that wanted to sign up for that gig. One night, we had two women who were lesbians working and they trespassed him because he was carrying something. They gave him a warning. He came back again and they arrested him. Everybody in the street was singing that song "Na, na, na, na, hey, hey, goodbye" to this guy. One officer said later, "I couldn't look at you because I would have started laughing. It would have been incredibly unprofessional." That went

> on for years, the battle with him, and then he disappeared. After that there were no problems.

Dorothy Abbot directed programming for the festival until 1996, and K. J. Mohr stepped in later to become a lynchpin for many years. With help from them and others, the festival went from showing five films and selling 1,850 tickets in 1990 to showing thirty-seven films in 1999, reaching the milestone of "ten straight years of queer cinema" with about 15,000 in attendance. In 2013, the festival showed ninety films from around the world. Tampa Theatre proved to be an ideal home where the audience could relax and be themselves.

Puig recalled the boost the festival brought to Tampa Theatre.

> It was a huge moneymaker for the theater because gays and lesbians know how to drink, and we told them [at the theater], "You need to order more vodka." They didn't, and they ran out. The bartenders loved it because our

In 2006, the Tampa International Gay and Lesbian Film Festival celebrated Tampa Theatre's eightieth birthday with an elaborate cake. Tampa Theatre.

K. J. Mohr and Renee Cossette, longtime organizers of the Tampa International Gay and Lesbian Film Festival. 2014. Courtesy of Renee Cossette and Nick Cardello Photography.

> community knows how to tip. Such excitement during those festivals. Single people and couples who really didn't like to go to the clubs and the bars, this was something else they could do.

Festival director Renee Cossette recalled the time the festival was held elsewhere:

> One year, we did not come here to the Tampa Theatre. We had an executive director at the time, he said, "We can't afford it. It's too big. Let's go somewhere else." We paid for that. Our audience was very, very angry because we have a lot of couples that met here; they met at the festival, and the Tampa Theatre is their home. When they found out, they were extremely upset. They were just livid.

Rediscovering History

Despite the marketing of Tampa Theatre's heritage as a vintage movie palace, there had never been an organized effort to document its history or preserve its records. It seemed as if old customers and employees would always be around and details of the palace's past forever in easy reach. It often takes outsiders to see local landmarks in a new light and look beyond local legends for a deeper truth. In her role working with the public as the theater's marketing director, Tara Schroeder became acquainted with patrons and learned of their deep attachment to the place.

> I was immensely entertained with stories people would tell me about their experiences here. I thought the stories should be collected and saved. I got a grant to do a little booklet to print them. I think it was called "Movie Palace Magic." I really didn't have the bandwidth to commit to that project, but I just did what I could. Fortunately, Janna Jones, who I met at Tampa Theatre, [joined the effort]. We had a conversation at the concession stand. She was interested in film and liminal places, particularly movie palaces, and she was searching for a dissertation topic. We started talking, and then it just blossomed from there. We were soliciting stories with signage and on the website and things. I would accompany Janna on her interviews with people, which was super-fun.

A tour with director of marketing Tara Schroeder (*left*) was a life-changing experience for Janna Jones. Tampa Theatre became a scholarly muse and set the stage for Jones's career in academia, circa 1995. Tampa Theatre.

Schroeder was able to connect with Blondelle Gladney in 1996 through the Tampa Theatre Stories Project. In a recorded oral history Gladney recounted memories dating back to the 1920s. 1995. Tampa Theatre.

For doctoral student Janna Jones, taking a tour of Tampa Theatre with Schroeder was a life-changing experience.

> I got my PhD at USF [University of South Florida]. I was still in class working my program in the Department of Communication, which was heavily ethnographic at the time. I was well trained to go in. I was ambitious, but I never thought about it that way. I had been writing about spaces, the biosphere in southern Arizona, bomb shelters, some interior design stuff.
>
> I took a tour with Tara. As often is the case in my life, I just understood that *this was it,* you know? I started as a kind of archivist for the Tampa Theatre, collecting information. Basically, Tara said, "Here's some boxes of stuff," and that's how it started. I just started organizing things. The summertime when I got started working on it at Tampa Theatre, those are some of my happiest days. That was 1996, I guess. I was able to spend so much time there and they let me in for free. From '96 to 2006, I was there all the time. It's just so beautiful to me when it's quiet and dark. It changed my life. It made my life so much better. I ended up writing my dissertation, then it was a big part of my first book, *The Southern Movie Palace.*
>
> I was looking at the theater as a portal for the city, and I felt like I could read it. If I could read the theater I would understand Tampa, particularly downtown. The interesting part to me was that it was a theater in the early years that did not allow African Americans inside. That part of the story wasn't getting preserved. Understandably, it's not what people wanted to preserve. The fact that it had been a segregated space wasn't part of the preservation. That became the centerpiece for what I was doing.

Jones found the connections through Tampa Theatre pivotal in her work.

> I went on to become a professor at USF. My first book is *The Southern Movie Palace.* I remember sitting in the Tampa Theatre with Tara, trying to figure out what other theaters I should study because I wanted to focus on the South. I traveled a lot to Durham, North Carolina, Atlanta, Memphis, Biloxi, Birmingham. I think that Tampa Theatre was the only theater of those that African Americans weren't allowed in at all. The other ones had balconies that they were allowed to enter by a side door.
>
> My timing was really good because the people that were working there in

the twenties were still alive. They're all long gone now. I didn't realize that at the time, I was just doing my work. But I'm so grateful that I was able to capture what I did when I did. I was so fortunate that so many people were willing to talk to me about some challenging subjects.

The Comfort of Strangers

Steve and Dianne Persall have a long history with Tampa Theatre. Steve's role as a movie critic meant he visited often for review screenings, sometimes with his wife, Dianne. Their relationship with the place is very personal, too. Their passion for cinema and one another found a favorite haunt when they visited Tampa Theatre together for the first time.

STEVE: Our first date was a nineties art movie starring Christopher Walken, *Comfort of Strangers* [1990]. It was supposed to be a very serious, earnest, dour, downbeat type of movie. He says "My father had a black mustache" four or five times in the movie. By the third time we're snickering. By the fourth time we're laughing. By the fifth time we were in love. We ended up laughing our way through the movie and then went to the old Hub [bar next to the theater] for a couple of drinks. By the end of the night, I told her I was gonna marry her. We talked pretty much everything out that night.

DIANNE: Our tenth anniversary we came because *Zardoz* [1974] was screening. There were like six of us in there. We're just laughing, goofing.

STEVE: Tara Schroeder was a *Zardoz* fan also. We sat there and just cracked up laughing through the entire thing. It was a good night.

We were part of the scare team when you used to have the haunted Halloween where you come jumping out and scaring people. They would set

For Dianne and Steve Persall, Tampa Theatre is an important touchstone in their relationship. Here they cavort at a Halloween costume party in 1998. Tampa Theatre.

Tampa Theatre has a reputation for sparking and sustaining romance. Long after coming to Tampa Theatre on their first date, the Persalls celebrated their twenty-fifth wedding anniversary by renewing their vows onstage. 2018. Courtesy of Steve Persall.

up a little backstage tour, but each dressing room would have a ghoul or two in there. That was a lot of fun.

They had a premiere of *Halloween H20* [1998]. It was the first sequel after years and years. They had a Michael Myers costume contest. Everybody came dressed with the mask and a machete, and I came dressed as Austin Powers.

DIANNE: It was a homemade costume. It was a yellow polyester thing and we found a wig.

STEVE: I won the costume contest that night, but I said, "Well, I've got a confession to make, I'm not really Mike Myers, I'm Steve Persall from the *St. Petersburg Times*."

DIANNE: One of the nice things with Tampa Theatre, particularly when you were the movie critic before you had streaming, we had a lot of different selections. This was one of the few places where you could see a lot of the independent films, a lot of the Oscar films, and other things that weren't getting picked up by the big theaters. You either had to catch it here or just wait until it came out on DVD.

STEVE: I've been participating in the Summer Movie Classics since 1993. It's a chance for, I'll be honest, some old timers like me and Bob Ross, Harriet Deer, to show what we know. I did one talk after *Cool Hand Luke,* and I was telling Dianne on the way over, "People have seen this thing over and over again. There's not gonna be anyone," and the place was half full at least. And 90 percent of them stick around after the movie and 10 percent of them are really leaning forward or asking questions.

DIANNE: I think this also appeals to young people because even though you can get all this stuff on your phone, it's different than coming and being with people to see that. Even if they're choosing a movie they've already seen, they'll come back and see it as a group and enjoy it as an event. Or if we have live music or any of the other things. There's unique opportunities for that.

We used to do the sing-alongs, that was great. *Grease, Mary Poppins.* The one that that absolutely kills every time is *The Sound of Music* because you have people who sarcastically goof on it. Like someone came dressed as a mountain with little Barbie dolls, the costume contest. It was awesome. *Rocky Horror*. *Greatest Showman.* It's gonna sell out. They're gonna come and they're gonna sing with it. There's nothing quite like getting together with people to experience something. I actually think about the Tampa Theatre as a sacred space in that when you come, you know it's going to be something special.

STEVE: It's beautiful and in some areas, a little grotesque. Like the movies it shows, it has that range of impressions that it can make on you. Here's a theater that lets you luxuriate in it. Everybody who works here, everybody who gets involved here knows they have skin in a very important game. To have something like this as a movie provider but also as a historic monument, as everything else grows up around Tampa. Keep something here for us, please.

DIANNE: We've had our anniversaries here.

STEVE: We renewed our vows. One time by the Reverend John Bell.

DIANNE: For our twenty-fifth anniversary we had our names on the marquee.

STEVE: I called up John and they put it up on the marquee briefly [for the couple to pose in front of]. It was nice, and we have that framed and hanging in our dining room now.

Film Camp

As the communications director, Tara Schroeder was always keen to expand educational opportunities at the theater. "I was super interested in learning about the art behind the theater. I put together a lesson plan with a friend over at the Hillsborough County School Board and developed this program to have field trips. I can focus on whatever they need me to focus on," she said at the time. Catering to one-off field trips was satisfying, but Schroeder dreamed about something more fun and meaningful for children, like a film camp. A partnership with the Florida Center for Instructional Technology at the University of South Florida provided the needed support to create a summer film camp at the theater. James Welsh, then a postgraduate student focusing on literacy studies and media literacy, helped to build the curriculum.

Schroeder recalled proposing the idea to Roy Winkelman, the center's director.

> Roy Winkelman had a long history with the theater. I said, "I have this crazy idea. We got the place, you got the toys and the teachers, you want to have some fun?" And he said, "Sure. Let's try it." James Welsh was completing his dissertation and working for Roy at the same time. He and I got to be kind of the mom and dad and we figured it out as we went along.

Welsh described the beginnings from his perspective of his role: "The FCIT staff basically just loaded up all of our video cameras and laptops and brought it down. Everybody worked as camp counselors with the kids. We all come from K-12 and technology, so we had people who were video editors, graphic artists, creative people. We worked on creating a curriculum."

During the course of the week, the counselors would help the kids form groups. Together, each group would write, perform, film, and edit an original movie. On the last day of camp, the parents would attend a screening of the finished products with their children.

Welsh described the film camp's early success.

James Welsh was the mastermind behind the curriculum of Tampa Theatre's summer film camp. 2004. Tampa Theatre.

> The first camp was summer of 2004. Downtown was kind of a wasteland. YouTube didn't exist. There were no iPhones, all of those things that now make visual storytelling so much more accessible, those things didn't exist. We had no idea if it was even a possibility to have a finished product at the end of a week. We worked with the kids that first week and it started looking good. As it got later in the week, we contacted the parents and let them know we're going to screen their films on Friday. At the end of the first week that summer, the kids had had a good time. It worked out great for everybody.

From there the film camp expanded, Welsh said.

> We started hiring classroom teachers to come and work at the camp, so there's all of this extra experience and knowledge about classroom management, about pedagogy, about teaching that comes into play. Each year, we would expand what we did, change our approach, incorporate ideas from the educators. We always felt like the camp is more about teaching communication and collaboration than it is about teaching technical filmmaking. We're giving them the basics of visual storytelling. We talk about shots and angles, framing, editing shots, sequences and scenes into a larger project. There's no test at the end.

> The kids don't make the content decisions that we would necessarily choose for them. They do a lot of pop culture references, a lot of ghost stories, a lot of creativity and energy. From the beginning, when somebody comes up with an unacceptable idea, we say, "On Friday, you're going to be sitting here and your parents are going to be next to you, and what you're filming will be on the screen." We came up with some limits, no blood, no weapons, which started off as no guns but once we said no guns, a lot of knives started showing up. A lot of swords. Us trying to direct them away from absolute massacres is part of the camp.
>
> There are many different ways to be successful in this camp. There are kids who don't care about being on camera. They want to direct the camera. There are kids who come in, believe it or not, who really only care about script writing, or kids that really only care about editing. Filmmaking takes a community of people with lots of different talents. It's bigger than any individual. There are kids who came here as third graders who then came back every summer all the way through ending high school. Then after graduation, kids who still come as volunteers, and we refer to them as production assistants. I was the camp director for a number of years. It's been the biggest joy to see how it's grown.

The campers' selections of characters and themes have been entertaining, Welsh said.

> We have a whole series on a character called Detective Clumsy that one group created. Every summer, they would sign up for the same week, so they'd come back and do another Detective Clumsy film. We had a group one year who wrote a movie called *Candy Heist.* They wrote a script with a candy heist where they break into the vault at Tampa Theatre to get the candy. Part of their motivation was that they had to eat a bunch of candy to make this movie. It was a movie about a candy heist that was really a candy heist.

Communications director Jill Witecki said she found a film-camp moment useful in her work: "Whenever I try to explain to people what film camp is, this is one of the stories I tell. Walking in the front door of the theater one shoot day and this kid dressed as predator, from *Alien vs. Predator,* went streaking through the lobby being pursued by a kid dressed as a banana. I would buy a ticket to that."

Josh Morgan (in the orange shirt) during stop-motion animation week of summer film camp 2015. He went on to become a film-camp counselor, study filmmaking in college, and pursue filmmaking professionally.

Besides having fun, campers benefited in other ways, Welsh said.

> I was just thinking of a kid whose mom told me how important this camp was to him because he never felt like he fit in at school. He got teased and he just never found his group. He found them here. This was the thing that he looked forward to all year long. It unlocked something for him. He really pushed it too with some of the stuff that he created here. He was trying to be the David Lynch of film camp with a vision of what he wanted to create.

The theater itself has played a role too, Welsh explained.

> If you were sitting in a conference room somewhere watching your movie projected, it's not the same. This place has a history. People have been enjoy-

above No day of programming better encapsulates Tampa Theatre's unique place in the community than Halloween 1996. It hosted a campaign stop for a presidential hopeful and a raucous sing-along screening of *The Rocky Horror Picture Show*. Tampa Theatre.

right Barry Bostwick (*top row, center*), who played "Brad Majors" in the 1975 film, joined local actors from the *Beyond Any Measure* shadow cast for a special presentation of *The Rocky Horror Picture Show* in 2019. Tampa Theatre.

In 1996, Republican presidential candidate Bob Dole (with red tie) stumped at Tampa Theatre, joined by Senator Dick Gephart (*left*) and former President George H. W. Bush (*right*). Tampa Theatre.

ing films in that space for a hundred years. Your film is one of those on the big screen. Tampa Theatre is an amazing resource for the entire community. The reason it exists, at least in part, is because the people of Tampa value it. The kids that we started off with are voting. We want to make sure that those kids leave here with an appreciation of what this is as a cultural resource. I was able to spend time here as a kid. It's a magical place.

Overture

More than a century after opening, nothing rocks Tampa Theatre to life like the Mighty Wurlitzer organ, which requires no speakers or amplification. When most people see the musician seated on the stage at the keys of this titan, they have no idea that they are only seeing the Wurlitzer's control console. The instrument itself, the part that makes all of the sound, is artfully hidden in the theater's walls, enfolded in faux balconies and decorative designs. Before the instrument is even played, one can hear the hushed rumble of the organ's fans priming its pipes with a steady flow of air. The rich sound of the instrument is like an orchestra in the hands of the right artist. Accompanying a film with the Wurlitzer organ is a highly distinct and demanding discipline.

It may seem like a novelty to visit a theater to see a silent film with live music from a Wurlitzer organ, but the experience is essential to early cinema and the theater itself. "When we replicate that experience today," John Bell said, "the first-timers who've never seen a silent film properly, in a movie palace with live musical accompaniment, are just blown away because it's a completely different art form. I tell people don't ever watch a silent film on television because it's terrible. It's not nearly the same experience."

A good player elevates the film, giving a sense of immediacy to the drama on screen. The restoration of the instrument had been one of Bell's first major accomplishments after taking on the theater's directorship in 1985. Under his leadership, silent film became part of the Tampa Theatre's identity again, cultivating a dedicated audience through quality programming, talented organists, and a little show business panache.

None of it would be possible without musicians and technicians trained for the pipe organ; they usually volunteer their services, primarily for the thrill of playing the beastly contraption. These days, finding a vintage instrument in an original movie palace is even more difficult than finding players, so musicians in the know seek out gems like Tampa Theatre. Bob Baker, who played often during the 1990s and 2000s, used to joke, "I get paid in all the popcorn I can eat." Of course, he came for his love of music and the antique instrument. He taught himself to play the organ at age eight and wanted to live a life of music. He had worked as a musical therapist in correctional facilities before moving to Florida to take a regular gig at the Venice Country Club as resident organist. He found Tampa Theatre's Wurlitzer and couldn't resist. In 2009, Baker passed away hours after a performance.

In 2002, volunteer organist Bob Courtney talked about the thrill of performing, saying, "You start playing, the spotlights come on, you push that button [which raises the organ to stage level], and up you come. It's always amazing to get that organ going good and then bring it up. To me, nothing is more thrilling. People love it. It's kind of an ego builder." He loved to play at screenings of classic films the most.

In some cases, the Wurlitzer's music has been an agent of healing. Johnnie June Carter was drawn to the piano and organ at a young age. When her father died suddenly in 1973, the girl found she no longer enjoyed playing as she did before. For twenty-seven years, she could not play a note. During a tour of Tampa Theatre, she was invited to play the organ, an instrument she had not heard live since she was a teen. The sound reawakened her musical appetite, and she soon went on a quest to buy a theater organ to be installed in her home in Wimauma, Florida. It took an eighteen-wheel tractor trailer to ship it down, and a team of three men took ten days to construct it. The pipes alone filled a large room, and another was occupied with a giant air blower. She turned her music room into a theater where she could entertain. Michael Kent designed the room to evoke Tampa Theatre, saying, "We couldn't duplicate it because that would have cost hundreds of thousands of dollars." After her life had been upended by the joyous sounds of the theater organ, Carter confessed in 2006, "Everything I have is either gone into this organ or will go into it, but I have no regrets. I plan to live to be over a hundred so I can get my money's worth." In addition to her own instruments at home, perhaps Carter's greatest thrill was playing Tampa Theatre's Wurlitzer before features.

Coming Up Rosa

Rosa Rio always had a clear vision of herself. The exact year of her birth in New Orleans would later be the subject of much speculation. Named Elizabeth Raub by her parents, Rio was naturally gifted as a pianist, playing by ear at age four. As a precocious eight-year-old, she announced her personal mission statement: "When I grow up, I want to play a big piano, wear pretty clothes and lots of jewelry, and make people happy." The child prodigy was lavished with attention for her talents. As she matured, she applied herself to the study of music and her ambitions grew with her first lesson at age eight. "I thought I couldn't be bothered with the baby stuff when I could play the real big stuff like 'Alexander's Ragtime Band,'" she said. "It was the most valuable lesson that I never got over. To this day, I still want to learn."

Her parents had always been supportive of Rio's music but only in situations they found to be socially acceptable for a girl, which were limited to religious performances and minor social occasions. She played her first paid gig at the tender age of ten, filling in for a friend at a theater for a nickel an hour. With a loud projector in the venue, her friend advised her to play fast and loud to drown out the noise. Her performance was interrupted by her angry father. "He took me right out of there," she remembered, "saying that no daughter of his would do that kind of work." To their credit, Rio's parents sent her to study music education at Oberlin College, but her spirit rebelled against the promise of a quiet, staid life as a music teacher.

She soon answered the call of the Mighty Wurlitzer. While visiting her aunt in Cleveland on spring break, Rio visited a movie palace for the first time. "I had never seen anything like the velvet draperies, gold, and glitter. I thought I was going to see a show. Instead, it was an organ that I heard and a spotlight that grew larger and larger. The organ came up on a lift, which I had never seen. I was floored. My eyes and ears exploded. I was bitten." At last, Rio had found a setting and an instrument that matched her lofty ambitions as a performer and an artist. The theater organ, and the Wurlitzer in particular, was the most glamorous instrument of the age. Perhaps most importantly for Rio, it was impossible to ignore.

Rio quickly enrolled at the Eastman School of Music in Rochester, New York, to learn the art of motion picture accompaniment. After graduation, she promptly got her first real theater gig in her hometown of New Orleans. She played all day, 11:30 a.m. until 11 p.m., seven days a week for the handsome wage of forty dollars a week. Theater organs had reached a fever pitch at the time, and good players were in high demand. Rio chose her stage name because it could always fit on a theater marquee.

Rio explained that she prepared to accompany a film by planning cues and themes around each scene.

> First, I view the silent picture, then I decide on the themes: character, love, dramatic, suspense, mysterioso, hurry, agitato, strings. When I write my cue sheet, the lineups are for title inserts, scenes, timing, type of music, and so forth. I memorized the main themes and rely on my ability to improvise—not fake—the correct music for each scene, hence my eyes stay on the screen and not on the music rack.

Rio set her sights on a position at Loew's theaters in New York, one of the most competitive markets in the country. She opened the Burnside Theater in Brooklyn, playing a Moller organ with an orchestra and as a soloist. Rio nourished her appetite for learning and sought out Joseph Schillinger, who took a mathematical approach to music. The teacher had molded great talents such as Glenn Miller, Jesse Crawford, and George Gershwin.

Rio's return to New Orleans must have felt like a triumphant homecoming. She had married a music professor from Eastman, appropriately named John Hammond. They both worked at the illustrious Saenger Theatre, an atmospheric

Rosa Rio playing at the Burnside Theater in Brooklyn, circa 1926. Courtesy of Rosa Rio.

opened in 1927. That same year, she was a touring organist in the Saenger theater chain when an innovative film called *The Jazz Singer* arrived and talkies began to take over. The sound of Al Jolson's voice caused her to break down crying at the implications for her craft. Although Rio had returned to her hometown, she never seemed to have entertained the idea of settling down into a domestic routine, even after giving birth to a son and divorcing. Before long, she was breaking down barriers at the Brooklyn Fox Theater as the first female organist. She earned a reputation in the industry as being an excellent accompanist and improviser.

When the demand for theater organs collapsed in the 1930s, Rio earned a living as a vocal coach, but she missed performing. She found salvation in soap operas. The NBC Radio Network needed musicians to accompany their expansive lineup of daytime dramas.

Bell picked up the story.

> Rosa got a call that the organist was sick, and could she come substitute to play with the orchestra in the radio studio? She played and she did fine. The original organist passed away I think, so she stayed a little longer, but she still wasn't given the job permanently. She finally went up to the manager and said, "Excuse me, why are you still looking for an organist? 'Cause I'm here." The manager said, "Well, we were kind of looking for a man." Without missing a beat, she said, "Well, are you looking for a man or are you looking for an organist?"

Rio was the first woman to be hired into an orchestra of 156 men, and she stayed twenty-two years. Rio became the Queen of the Soaps, running between studios to play in several series a day. She recounted, "I had to keep my eyes on the script, director, clock, and the actors all at one time." Rio worked with a cavalcade of Tinseltown stars during her radio years. She worked with young theatrical dynamo Orson Welles when he played *The Shadow* in 1937–1938. "Orson Welles was young and new at the game," Rio recalled. "He was absolutely fabulous to work with and very funny. He would do impromptu sketches during intermission and have us all in stitches." Rio's unsettling accompaniment enhanced the show's eerie air. She devoted her talent to the war effort during World War II. A wartime program called "Rosa Rio Rhythms" served as a morale-booster for troops serving overseas. She performed live shows for servicemen recovering in military hospitals. "Music was a therapy," she said. "The two most requested songs were 'Begin the Beguine' and 'Stardust.'"

In 1948, she married fellow organist and manager Bill Yeoman, who was her partner in music and business. Rio played for television studios but found it less rewarding, probably because there was less room for spontaneity. Her TV credits include *The Today Show, Guiding Light,* and *As the World Turns.* In 1960, the couple relocated to Connecticut, where they opened a studio for music and vocal instruction.

Most people move to Sun City Center in Florida to retire, but for Rosa Rio, who moved there in the mid-1990s, giving up the pleasures of playing and performing was unthinkable. The couple's new Florida home accommodated a nine-foot Baldwin concert grand, a Rodgers theater organ, and a Hammond organ. Her presence at a meeting of the Central Florida Theater Organ Society lit up the room as the members gathered at Tampa Theatre realized they were in the presence of a living legend.

Bell recalled that meeting.

> I met Rosa in the late nineties, and I remember she was standing at the back of the hall. She was here for an event that was featuring the theater organ, and someone introduced me to her. That's when she came to Tampa Theatre for the first time. When she went to play the Wurlitzer after a show it was amazing. She sat at the theater organ and said, "Oh, I think I played this instrument." It turns out she started her career accompanying silent films in New York [where parts of the instrument came from]. She was a very accomplished organist, and she was a trailblazer. As I got to know her through the years, I was just amazed. She would tell the best stories.

Rio played her first silent film at Tampa Theatre in 1996. The pairing seemed natural and somehow inevitable, especially considering the similarities between

Tampa Theatre and the Saenger in her birthplace of New Orleans, another atmospheric design by John Eberson where she played early in her career.

Tara Schroeder said,

> That started a long relationship. She could do media like nobody's business. She enchanted whoever was doing the interview, flirted with the men shamelessly, they all loved her. She was a masterful genius with silent film accompaniment. She could've just sat on her laurels, but what brought her happiness was connecting with the audience. And doing little things. Little snippets of music that would get put underneath a score. Like *Phantom of the Opera,* when the Phantom is underwater with a straw, you'd hear a couple little snippets of *Yellow Submarine.* Once Rosa hit the scene the audiences grew and grew because of her and the experience.

In Rio's hands, the Wurlitzer and Tampa Theatre came to life, demonstrating the immediacy of live cinema. Her Tampa debut drew two hundred. Attendance grew from there. A Buster Keaton double feature packed the house three years later, selling 1,250 tickets. Rosa wanted the audience to be active participants in the movie, not passive spectators. "You can applaud or hiss if you want," she would say. Every show ended with a standing ovation. And then she raced out to the lobby to meet her fans and sign autographs. Volunteer usher Betsy King recalled, "She told us wonderful, rather scandalous stories."

Bell also lauded Rio's magnetic presence at the theater.

> Rosa was just remarkable. She became a rock star. Anytime we would have Rosa Rio onstage performing for a silent film, the theater was absolutely packed. We would sell out all of these shows. Buses from Sun City would arrive. She would write new scores for the silent films that we would show. I remain anxious about every detail of a silent film presentation until Rosa takes over. Once Rosa began playing her signature opener, "Everything Is Coming Up Roses" during her set before the movie, I knew I could relax because it's her show and it's time to sit back and enjoy the ride.

Rio exalted the role of the theater organ like few could, saying, "Mood music creates the emotional part, which is most important. Theaters used to use orchestras

for background music, but they could never, ever cue it the way a single musician can at the organ. The color of the music creates the situation. Make the viewer feel the tension of the situation."

Rio even found occasion to spook her audience, like a now-legendary showing of *Nosferatu* in 2000 that drew nine hundred patrons. Roddy King was at that presentation and vividly recalled the occasion. "I'll never forget Rosa Rio and the Halloween special," he said. "They had the organ come up and you could hear it playing but there was nobody there. It's playing very spooky type music." Then came the surprise: "These guys bring out a casket from the back, and set it down, right next to the organ. They open the casket and Rosa Rio steps out."

Schroeder explained, "We have 'Toccata' *and* 'Fugue in D Minor' bellowing throughout the theater and there's nobody on the organ. We did the smoke and everything. Then the curtains part. I had pallbearers bring a coffin out."

Rosa Rio moved to Florida to retire after an amazing musical career, but instead she began a new chapter at Tampa Theatre. 2006. Tampa Theatre.

Enveloped in a large, blood-red scarf, Rio stepped out of the coffin to begin the show.

On the subject of her age, Rio liked to keep people guessing. "Age is a number," she would quip, "and mine's unlisted." The jokes made light of the fear of being passed over for work because of her age. As a female entertainer, she felt especially vulnerable to age discrimination and never celebrated her birthday. As she neared the end of her life, she considered revealing her age at last at a show in 2007 called "Silent Clowns Comedy Shorts," a matinee held on her birthday. Schroeder remembered, "She said she was going to announce how old she was. Then at the last minute, she decided she wasn't. Then she gets out on stage and she decides, 'Okay, I'm gonna do it,' and announces she's a hundred and five." For her part, Rio said she felt blessed to have had such a fruitful career and for ending her century of song at Tampa Theatre, where she accompanied films more than thirty times.

Rio said,

> I never got over the glee of when I heard the first theater organ. I still have that feeling, it's still a part of me. I can't believe that I've been so fortunate to have been in so many things that went out and I bounced back. The word retire is not in my vocabulary. I pinch myself at having come full circle doing what I've loved most. I was born with a show business ego. I have such gratitude for the wonderful people who have love for the theater organ, silent pictures, and Tampa Theatre. My dream came true. I'm truly blessed.

Rio broke her hip in 2010, but her husband, Bill Yeoman, said an intestinal flu exhausted her in the end. On her deathbed, she told him, "Daddy, I want to go. Don't stop me." In memory, Tampa Theatre showed her favorite film, *The Play House,* with Steven Ball on organ. Ball, a scholar of music and the organ, was one of her last proteges. At the conclusion of the performance, a spotlight lingered on the console and the three roses left on the organ bench. The audience gave Rosa Rio one more standing ovation.

5

Spirit in the Dark

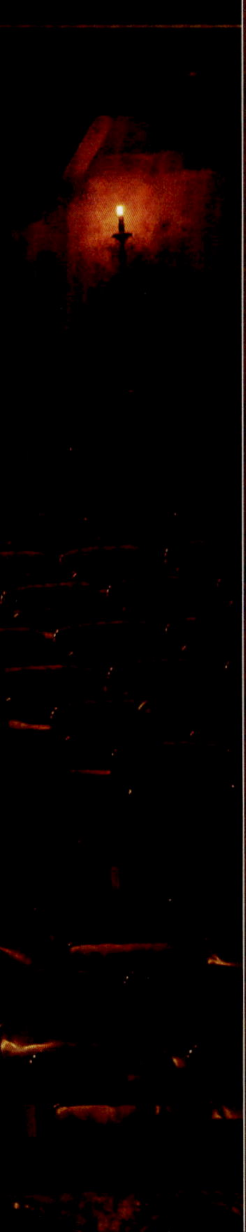

The first ghost stories began after the death of a longtime projectionist. Strange incidents have occurred in and around the projection booth ever since. Tampa Theatre.

In the years since its rescue, the theater went from luring the press with spooky stories each Halloween to managing throngs of ghost hunters who plead to spend the night and scour the theater for lingering spirits. Tampa Theatre's ghost stories began as curiosities, usually during Halloween, but they come from a real place. Too many theater associates told of eerily similar experiences to be dismissed.

Tampa Theatre's best-known employee only found fame after his death. Coworkers described Foster "Fink" Finley as an unremarkable presence in life: short and thin, balding and with bloodshot eyes, a lifelong bachelor and devotee of cigarettes, coffee, and dry humor. He carved out his niche in the projectionist booth, a role that was comfortably remote for the semirecluse. In the 1920s, Finley had proven himself as a projectionist at the Strand, Bonita, and Victory theaters. He worked his way up the Publix Theatres chain to Tampa Theatre in 1930 and did not leave his post until his death in 1965.

For thirty-five years, Finley arrived for work long before opening to perform a quiet morning ritual. His booth, which included a private restroom, became a home away from home where he shaved and dressed for work each day. His position did not require him to wear a formal suit during working hours, but he always donned one out of a sense of pride. Stage crew member Syd Morris said, "Fink was a bachelor, and the job was the only thing that meant anything to him. Fink was a good man; he was just a little strange. He was married to the job and to the building. He worked here right up till just before he died, after the theater started going downhill in the sixties."

Thirty-five years cloistered in a poorly ventilated projectionist's booth had ruined Finley's health. The carbon arc lamps used in old projectors produced a superfine powdery ash that coated every surface of the booth as well as the lungs of anyone nearby. Projectionists often suffered from black lung as a result of being confined with the substance for up to twelve hours at a time in unventilated spaces. Gary Ratliff explained, "Floating around free, it's a fine gray powder, almost like talcum

As part of its ghost tour program, Tampa Theatre commissioned a series of portraits by local artist Shane Douberly, including this one of spectral projectionist Fink Finley. Tampa Theatre.

powder." Congress eventually passed a law requiring better ventilation in projection booths. Finley's constant cigarette smoking only made matters worse.

Finley continued to work with the same dedication after his cancer diagnosis. Toward the end, it took him about twenty minutes to climb the stairs to reach the booth for work each day. He died at home two weeks after collapsing in the booth. His old partner in projection Bill Hunt was the first to notice the strange occurrences in the booth after Fink's passing. Other reports soon followed. Hunt said, "His apartment was just a place where he slept. His real and only home was the Tampa Theatre. If there is such a thing as a ghost, I think it would surely be there. He loved the place just that much."

Schroeder recounted an early tale from the booth: "The projectionist who replaced him didn't last long. There was a heavy door up there that opened and closed at will, and a toggle switch on the projector would go on and off. He even saw apparitions in his peripheral vision. Of course, no one was there."

Schroeder's successor Jill Witecki told another: "As the projectionist would be standing at the window here, watching for those little cue dots indicating that it was time to switch the reels, they would feel somebody tap them on the shoulder like they were saying, 'Pay attention. Here it comes.' Nothing will ruin your concentration faster than getting tapped on the shoulder when you're the only one in the room."

Projectionist Bobby Pratt remembered that whenever he waited for his cue, he would hear the heavy generator room door open and slam shut nearby. He saw a shadow out of the corner of his eye and felt a presence. Gary Ratliff recalled how even the most unfazed workers experienced strange incidents in the old booth: "Frank Montgomery and Curtis Schneider weren't necessarily superstitious or scared, but they said every once in a while weird things happened. They'd see something peripherally, and they just didn't know what it was." Bell explained, "They began to realize this is probably Fink because he was known as a practical joker in life."

Witecki said she heard stories from the theater's guests as well as its workers after Finley died.

Ever since then, pretty much every projectionist we've had has had stories up there that lead them to believe that Fink is probably still coming to work six days a week. It wasn't just the projectionists. Guests out on the balcony were having experiences, usually involving smells [such as coffee and cigarettes]. The one that was the hardest to explain was the lingering smell of lilac over and over again. Over the years, we have gotten people telling us that they smell lilac when they're sitting up in the balcony. A guest on a tour suggested that the popular aftershave back in Fink's time [Pinaud Clubman's] was Lilac Vegetal. Maybe what we're smelling is Fink having his morning shave up here every day. We had to order some off Amazon and smell it. That is what the smell is up here. It's that weird powdery lilac scent.

The first newspaper stories devoted to Fink's ghost appeared during the 1970s. Popular interest in the paranormal was at a new height at the time, in part as a result of haunted Hollywood hits such as *The Exorcist* (1973) and *Amityville Horror* (1979). Stories of the projectionist became established lore over the years, and the status of the legend grew from there. As a savvy communications director, Schroeder saw the ghost stories as a marketing opportunity. She explained,

When I got down to Tampa, everybody said Tampa Theatre is haunted. Fink was identified long before I got there. Around Halloween, everybody wants to do a story on the ghost of Tampa Theatre. Then we started doing ghost tours, realizing, "Oh, you can make a dime on ghosts." There was a guy named Scott Harrell who wrote for [alt-weekly newspaper] *Creative Loafing*. Scott was writing a story on the ghost of Tampa Theatre, and he thought it would be fun to spend a night there. I met him after a film screening one night, it was about nine o'clock. I showed him where the beer tap was, I said, "Here's my home number. I live up the street. Call me if anything goes on." I said "Bye, bye. See you later." And then I snuck in a back door of the theater. I hung out for a while and just messed with him.

I didn't hear from him. The next day I called the newsroom and he wasn't there. I talked to his editor. I thought for sure he would see through my ruse. She's like, "I don't know what happened. He was completely frightened." I said, "Wait, he doesn't know that was me?" And she said, "No, he came in just completely freaked out." I said, "Oh gosh." I kind of felt bad for alarming him. Then she said, "Let's let him write the story." So, he wrote the story and she

> kept tabs on it. When he turned it in, and it was done, I called him. I was like, "Dude, you know it was me, right?" And then he was able to add an epilogue to the story.
>
> Paranormal investigators were humping my leg left and right to come into the theater. But you know, you say yes to one and you have to say yes to all of them and that was just too much to deal with. I did let one group in. They validated some of the things that were happening. We had a news crew in, a woman with a camera. She was doing the story on Tampa Theatre's ghost, and by the end of the visit, she physically ran out the front door because her camera was messing up and it completely rattled her. Realistically there's lots of funky wiring in that theater. Before rewiring, we had horrible problems if it was really quiet. There was a country music station that would come over the sound system, usually at inopportune times. And it was just because wires weren't shielded and signals in the air.

Following Schroeder as communications director, Jill Witecki continued the haunted theater theme.

> The ghost program was something that Tara did before I got here, but the stories have kind of grown and changed in the years that I've been doing the ghost tours. We do public tours in October and private tours for groups throughout the year. We go through the building, stop at six different locations, and tell some of the stories there. Tampa Theatre has the reputation as being one of the most haunted buildings in Tampa. I think there's a little bit of a misconception that people think if they're walking into a building that is haunted, that there must be people dying all the time in your building, and fortunately for us, that is not the case.

Bell said employees routinely invoke Finley's spirit. "We have embraced Fink because any theater worth its salt has a ghost," he said, "and we've got several. Fink is a good one, because he's a benign spirit. Today if something goes wrong in the building, if the server goes down, it's a building-wide Fink alert. We love Fink."

Paranormal investigators have helped the theater staff identify five other likely ghosts, all associated with certain parts of the building. Jeremy Rettig, who first became involved with the theater in 2012 as part of a paranormal research group,

Jeremy Rettig, the founder of Genesis Paranormal Services, has studied the building thoroughly and found several areas of interest including the projection booth. 2021. Jeff Fay.

above Florida natives Dan Myrick and Mike Monello introduce their new film, *The Blair Witch Project,* to a sold-out crowd in 1999. Tampa Theatre.

left Actor Ted Neeley appears at the Tampa Theatre stop on the *Jesus Christ Superstar* farewell tour in 2025. The actor sang along with the crowd from his seat. Jeff Fay.

said, "Jill was also working off of limited information. We knew some stories that had taken place, but we didn't know everything. We focused on some areas of interest." The information gathered by these investigations is anecdotal, but sustained research has yielded enough accumulated evidence to give skeptics pause. Repeating all of the details here is beyond the scope of this book and are best experienced in the semidark of the theater during a tour.

Even John Bell, who considers himself a skeptic, became a believer.

> It must have been one o'clock in the morning. I'm the only one left in the building. I'm finishing up the paperwork because I don't want to have to leave it until tomorrow. Then I realized when I'm about done, I left a receipt in an office downstairs. So, I go out my office door, go down the hallway, I get halfway down the stairs, and I hear, like thirty feet behind me, my office door slam shut. I looked at my watch and I said, "I should probably just go." I didn't even turn around. I just went straight out the door. Didn't bother to turn off any lights or anything. I figured it was Fink's way of telling me you need to go home. If you're stuck somewhere in the afterlife, this is not a bad place to hang out. I fully intend on haunting this place when I'm done.

The Juggler

In her early teens, Tara Schroeder went on a Girl Scout field trip to the Saenger Theatre in her hometown of New Orleans (the same as Rosa Rio's) and fell in love with the space. After completing her education, she landed a job as the communications director at the League of Historic American Theatres. There she first met John Bell and heard of Tampa Theatre, with its uncanny resemblance to the Saenger as an Eberson atmospheric. That led to her twenty-year tenure as the director of marketing and community relations, a role in which she was instrumental in elevating Tampa Theatre's profile.

Schroeder said,

> I was a national communications director [at the league], and Tampa Theatre was always my favorite little kid. It was so different from all of the other movie palaces and opera houses, and I just had an affection for that place before I even saw it. John Bell was on our board, and he was honestly one of my favorite board members. He had a great national reputation. He's a visionary.

Tara Schroeder was a transformational figure for Tampa Theatre. Her creative promotional efforts won the old palace many new friends. 2007. Tampa Theatre.

Tony Curtis made a special appearance at a screening of the comedy classic *Some Like It Hot* in 1996 as part of a tour organized by the National Film Registry to showcase its collection of classics. Curtis is photographed with Tara Schroeder (*left*) and her mother, Flora McCoy. Tampa Theatre.

When Bell asked Schroeder if she would join the team as Tampa Theatre's communications director in 1992, she accepted. In addition to her public relations duties, she coordinated volunteers, gave tours, and more. Bell, Schroeder, and programmer Diane Eberly were the theater's only office employees at the time.

Schroeder reflected on her early work there: "When I first arrived, Tampa Theatre was flying way under the radar. I would look for little one-offs that I could connect to different organizations in the community that would get more people in the theater. Sometimes we'd show films and three people would show up. I would say, 'Well, everybody that was there had a great time. Where were you?'"

Some films brought more audience engagement, Schroeder said.

> We did a film about Frank Lloyd Wright, so I reached out to the local American Institute of Architects. We got new people into the theater that way. We did a big premiere of *Much Ado about Nothing* with Kenneth Branagh and just made a big party out of it. It brought new people into the theater. There was a documentary called *The Sound and the Fury* [2000], which was

about cochlear implants. After the film, we had a discussion that got a little heated, and instead of hearing a lobby full of sound, I heard the sound of signing with hands, which was so amazing. There was a documentary called *Who Killed the Electric Car* [2006], and we got a gentleman who worked on the electric car to talk to us about his experience, about how they were pretty much shut down by the big guys. A man was almost in tears doing a film about Cuba and having a conversation with people and it got a little heated. I love that Tampa Theatre allowed opportunities for people to engage who may not or may agree.

Schroeder arranged the popular Spooktacular event beginning in 1991, following a Halloween film series by that name the previous couple of years. Although the theater no longer holds Spooktacular, it inspired a variety of Halloween-themed events every October.

Attendees at a screening of *The Wizard of Oz* in 2005. Tampa Theatre.

For many years, a cast of nasties turned the theater into a haunted house for Spooktacular events. Tampa Theatre.

The old, mysterious, and reportedly haunted theater is a natural for the Halloween season. 1992. *Tampa Tribune.*

Hollywood awards watch parties make guests feel like VIPs. Limo rides whisk them around the block to arrive for a walk on the red carpet. Tampa Theatre.

On Hollywood Awards Night, Pat Fenda (*far left*) plays the red-carpet gadfly Roan Jivers, greeting guests and providing a running commentary on fashion. Tampa Theatre.

> John gave me the flexibility to look for opportunities. Like Spooktacular, where we turned the whole theater into a haunted house and had to manage two hundred volunteers. There was this six-year-old kid that was coming out at the end, and he turned to his mom and said, "I want to go back." And just hearing that made it all worth it. I think large events that were outside of the normal programming helped to demonstrate Tampa Theatre's value and vitality to not only downtown, but Tampa and the Tampa Bay region.

Schroeder recalled other new endeavors that brought out more fans for Tampa Theatre.

> Oscar Night was another event that brought a lot of new people into the theater. We initially partnered with the Ronald McDonald House [charity]. It became clear that they needed to focus on their Storybook Ball, which was right on the heels of that. They ceded that license over to us. It was part of the Oscar Night America program, using the Oscars to allow local nonprofits to raise money.
>
> Oscar Night let you be a star. We gave people the visceral experience of jumping in a limousine, coming around the block, and being let out on the red carpet with the track lights and the red velvet ropes. We'd bring volunteer

FTS-ABC newscasters Martie Tucker and Brendan McLaughlin found themselves among characters at Oscar Night America 2001. Tampa Theatre.

At a sing-along screening of *The Sound of Music* in 2002, Charmian Carr (*center*), who played Liesel, was in attendance, photographed here with John Bell and Tara Schroeder. Tampa Theatre.

> high school kids into the fold as the screaming fans on the red carpet. And having the incomparable Pat Fenda. She was on the red carpet as "Roan Jivers" with a microphone and interviewing people as they got out of the limousine. I was her champagne wench and kept her filled. The red carpet that was specially designed for our sidewalk and then Roan Jivers putting a mic in your face, saying, "Oh my God, what are you *wearing*?" Having that element of letting people be part of the show and allowing women to wear their nice dresses outside brought a lot of new people into the theater.

Working with the media was another important aspect of Schroeder's job, she said.

> I was pitching stories and making friends with people in the media, which was really helpful. The feedback that I got from my friends in the media was they loved to do stories on the theater because I took care of them. I got them coffee, made sure everything was set up for them. I would do a lot of the groundwork in advance, coming up with questions, providing them with as much information as they needed. You can get your message out and help them have a good piece as well. Tampa Theatre became the media darling, both locally

Hollywood Awards Night, once known as Oscar Night America, makes a party out of watching the show. Tampa Theatre.

> and nationally. *Life Magazine* named it one of America's twenty-one wonders. Some of that national stuff, honestly, came through people that we knew at the League of Historic American Theatres. It deserves all those accolades.

Schroeder recalled her time at the theater with fondness.

> Tampa Theatre's special because it meets people where they are in a lot of different ways. So, whether you come to see concerts, or films, or just love the architecture, there's that connection on so many different levels. And then all the behind-the-scenes crazy stuff with the staff and the volunteers, cleaning popcorn or penguin poop off the carpet, and duking it out with drunk people at concerts. But that's a whole other story. My intention was just to have been there a few years and then make my way back to New Orleans. I was having so much fun I stayed for twenty.

With mixed emotions, Tara Schroeder relocated in 2012 to care for family, but her loving fingerprints are still quite evident. Thanks in large part to her marketing efforts and community contacts, Tampa Theatre went from being a well-kept local secret to attracting international attention and the support of influential friends.

Downtown Turnaround

Like a shimmering mirage on hot Florida asphalt, the vision of a thriving downtown Tampa always seemed to dissolve upon approach. When the area fell on hard times during the Great Depression, it faced a decade of wrenching decline. Few could have predicted that the second fall of downtown, which was well under way by the 1960s, would last about fifty years. In 1979, a local newspaper columnist could only dream of "brightly lit streets [and] hundreds of people in downtown Tampa attending conventions, or just milling about enjoying a lively sidewalk band before heading home to their high-rise apartment building on the Hillsborough River. Sounds like a different city." Boosters at the time predicted downtown's rebirth in the next seven to ten years, but it would take another forty, about as long as it took to build downtown in the first place.

In 1991, city leaders fretted over downtown's future. Woolworth's and Wolf Brothers had recently closed. Perhaps most crushing of all was the loss of the flagship Maas Brothers department store. Leland Cool, owner of the Nature Shop next

Downtown Tampa made an impressive rebound in the twenty-first century. Courtesy of the Tampa Downtown Partnership.

door to the theater, said, "It's getting worse year to year instead of getting better." The old Franklin Street Mall concept, which never caught on, seemed to be falling apart. City plans for the mall were predicated on downtown workers spending money they simply did not have. A report on the future of the Franklin Street Mall acknowledged that conditions would not be right for another ten years. City leaders had been trying to encourage ground-level retail in a downtown increasingly typified by glassy, faceless high-rises.

Very little had changed by 2000, when *St. Petersburg Times* journalist Sandra Thompson expressed concern for being panhandled while visiting Tampa Theatre.

> The problem is not the panhandler; the problem is there is nobody downtown at night, and because there is nobody downtown, many people won't come downtown. On a weekend night in Tampa, except for theatergoers, the north end of downtown is empty. Even the restaurant next door to the theater is now closed. I've often said I would have to leave Tampa if the Tampa Theatre ever closed. Buying the theater, a Rococo fairyland of a building, is one of the smartest things the city has ever done. It has consistently brought people downtown on weekend nights. And it's sitting there, all alone.

During the early 2000s, observers noted an encouraging uptick in weekend and evening traffic downtown. With attractions such as the convention center, Florida Aquarium, Amalie Arena, and the Straz Center for the Performing Arts, Tampa's inner city was gradually becoming a destination again. The business district's chang-

With a gradual opening that began in 2021, the Water Street development was a big boost to downtown Tampa. Courtesy of Keir Magoulas.

ing fortunes seemed to be manifested in the theater's neighboring property, which found more stable tenants beginning with Thai Corner in 2006.

Jeff Vinik will likely go down in history along with Henry Plant and Vicente Martínez Ybor as a transformational figure for Tampa. After buying the Tampa Bay Lightning hockey team in 2010, he saw opportunity in a long-neglected city. He aggressively bought up real estate around the Amalie Arena. His 56-acre Water Street development cost $3.5 billion to construct and sparked a much-needed downtown makeover. The concept included millions of square feet of retail and office space, an entertainment complex, more than five thousand condos and hotel rooms, and the University of South Florida's Morsani College of Medicine and Heart Institute. All of this activity coincided with heavy public investments in the area such as the Tampa Museum of Art, the Glazer Children's Museum, the Tampa Bay History Center, the Encore public housing development, and the RiverWalk. Tampa Theatre reminds visitors that beneath the veneer of recent construction, Tampa has a history worth exploring and preserving. Its vertical blade sign evokes the downtown of yesteryear and has become a local icon in the process.

Growing Up

John Bell said, "The theater first reopened [in 1977] under the auspices of the Arts Council of Tampa because the city was smart enough to say, 'We'll save the building and provide some support, but we don't know anything about operating a theater.' That arrangement stayed in place until 2010."

Tara Schroeder picked up the story of Bell and others raising the theater's prominence.

> John very expertly reached out into the community and pulled a great board together. One of those was Harrison Giddens. She had the foresight [that] instead of having the people of her generation get involved, she got the generation under that too. I think that helped propel Tampa Theatre forward. Our reputation grew as we started to have more presence in the community and the corporate world. I remember one of our first big fundraisers where there's all these people in the theater that had never been there before. They walked in and fell in love with it and were helping us move forward. I remember John and I standing there and thinking, "Our baby's growing up."

From Tampa Theatre's reopening in 1977, Harrison Giddens has been a tireless advocate. Tampa Theatre.

Tampa Theatre honored those who helped along the way in 2004 (*from left*), Harrison Giddens, Mary Kelly, Joan Jennewein, Martha Ferman, Charlie Miranda, and Mayor Bill Poe. Tampa Theatre.

Giddens remembered the early days in the 1980s when the board had to vote to buy "a can of paint." A fellow member likened the responsibilities and interlocking challenges of the board to "trying to pick up a pile of coat hangers from the bottom of your closet, and one is hooked to the next one."

Giddens credited Bell with her successes on the board.

> The people I have been privileged to serve with on the board have been extraordinary. John Bell and I came about the same time [mid-1980s], and that's been a wonderful walk. I got to know him during the first capital campaign. That was my first experience in learning how you really went about raising money. I learned that you have to earn the right to ask. I took so much more from the board than I gave. I learned so much from John. You get more emotional value out of something that you helped because you were a part of a team.

Board member Charlie Britton inspired the theater's leadership to think bigger. Tampa Theatre.

Tampa Theatre's marketing mixes glamour and humor, as this 2002 ad by the WestWayne Agency illustrates. Tampa Theatre.

In 2006, the theater and its supporters celebrated its eightieth birthday in style. Tampa Theatre.

During special events like WineFest, an extension of the stage allows guests to sip and dine under the stars. Tampa Theatre.

In 2001, the board and staff redoubled active efforts to raise money, leading the theater to hire its first director of development, J. L. Wagner. Banker and board chair Charlie Britton led a capital campaign soon after that, telling journalists, "Our fundraising effort is just a little beyond its infancy stage. This theater truly is a money pit. It's got to be a labor of love to keep the restoration going." Schroeder gave credit to Britton as "the one that came up with the idea for WineFest and called it Gone with the Wine. Our development director, J. L. Wagner, and the committee did a great job pulling that together from scratch and helping it to grow."

While planning for the theater's eightieth birthday in 2006, board member Giddens realized that the stage was a great fundraising asset that could be better leveraged. The theater created an extended stage designed to be easily installed, allowing more benefactors to sip and sup onstage under the stars.

WineFest began in 2002 as an annual fundraiser. While a featured movie played onscreen in the background at low volume, guests drank and mingled onstage. Cheeky variations of the movie titles supplied many memorable names for events, such as

Art Keeble (*right*) of the Tampa-Hillsborough Arts Council was an important partner for theater president John Bell. Tampa Theatre.

Raiders of the Lost Cork, The Grape Gatsby, Midnight in the Vineyard of Good and Evil, and Wine's World. Over the years, theater staff expanded on the wine tasting by adding a seminar for curious quaffers. Mise en Place, a fine-dining restaurant with chefs who always rose to the occasion, catered exquisite dinners inspired by that year's wines. Before long, WineFest lasted an entire weekend, with a wine tasting, wine-pairing dinner, and Sunday brunch. Board member Jeff Shear, a regular attendee, said, "My law firm typically buys a table and I invite people to come. I get calls from my friends, 'Hey, you got a table this year?' or, 'Did I make the invite list?'"

Bell described a period of expansion for the board.

> Between 1992 and 2010, Tampa Theatre Inc. grew every single year. We got more members who became more involved. In the early 2000s, we started doing some serious retreats. We brought in consultants. We really took the lid off of the board's thinking and began to have them think expansively about the theater, not just what it is and how to solve today's problems, but what can it be? What should it be? That was a very liberating and exciting exercise. Charlie Britton was encouraging us to think big. That began the momentum towards the realization that we really needed to spin away. We didn't want to divorce the Arts Council. We just wanted to grow up and leave home.

Giddens recalled Bell's dedication during lean times and growing pains: "I think about John. He must not have been able to sleep at night, when all of a sudden, the funds were cut off, and we were out there passing the plate. But look, look what's happened."

Bell explained how he persevered.

> I'm a firm believer that you can't force things. Things have to happen in their own time, for a reason. I'm pleased that the transition went so smoothly. We struck a new operating agreement with the City of Tampa. The city still owns the theater, but we have a long-term operating agreement to operate it on the behalf of the citizens.
>
> Nonprofit is just a tax status. It's not a business model. We like to show profit. The difference is in what happens to the profits. In the case of commercial cinema, those profits are given out to the shareholders. In the case of a nonprofit, we plow it right back into the theater, either into the facility or the mission of the organization.

Our budget is now almost five million dollars a year, but we have to raise more than a million dollars of that. It's great that 75 percent of our revenue is earned, but if we don't have those contributions coming in, people don't give and we don't get the grants, then we're losing a million dollars a year. Fortunately, we've found this formula and we're stable and got money in the bank.

The city helps to maintain the building. If we get to a point where we just can't figure something out, or something really major has gone wrong, then the city sends their folks and they come and help. Other partnerships are important: University of South Florida and their Department of Education; the Florida Center for Instructional Technology, which is the key partner behind our successful summer film camp; the Tampa Downtown Partnership has always been very supportive; all of our promoting partners, the community, nonprofit organizations, that we have an affinity with. We couldn't do any of what we do without those types of partnerships. In some ways, that speaks to the fact that when you're a mission-based community-centered organization, you can have those partnerships that are meaningful. It's not always about making money. It's about making the community a better place.

An Active Board

Jeff Shear's grandparents relocated to Tampa in 1926 for their honeymoon, a story told at the very beginning of this book. The newlyweds, both born in Philadelphia to Jewish immigrants, settled in Tampa, ran several businesses, and started a family. Jeff went to law school, specializing in real estate. He worked as the City of Tampa's assistant city attorney before going into private practice. Shear developed a lifelong relationship with Tampa Theatre, where his loves for family, fine art, and the legal profession all found a happy home.

Jeff Shear recalled,

I grew up on Davis Island, went to Gorrie Elementary School. I came to see *The Nutcracker* when I was in, probably first, second, third grade, something like that. That was probably my first real introduction that I remember to Tampa Theatre, was coming to see those shows. Obviously, that made a big impression on me and all my little classmates at the time.

Jeff Shear's background as a real estate attorney helped the theater navigate a crisis that could have shut it down. Tampa Theatre.

When I got to law school, I worked as an assistant city attorney, so I was involved with the City Council and knew Lee Duncan. Because of that, I always had an interest in the theater. I eventually made my way onto the board [in 2013] and have been serving on the board for ten-plus years. I served as chairman the last two years of the board [2021–2023] and still remain on. I've always felt a connection to Tampa Theatre. In later years, my wife and I enjoyed independent films, so we would come here often. My kids both went to film camp here, and we had my son's Bar Mitzvah party here at the theater.

This board is about keeping this building up and running and trying to improve it. It's all about raising money for that purpose. I was a little surprised when I first got more involved that we had trouble raising money, 'cause to me, Tampa Theatre is like old Tampa. You would have thought that this old Tampa money would have been pouring in. But for whatever reason that just wasn't in place. The theater had not been successful raising lots of money. Pretty soon after I got on the board was when we had our first big money raise to change out the seats and do some of the restoration work. We successfully got there on that one.

Another turning point for me was when we were able to get this big chunk of money from the CRA, the Community Redevelopment Agency. There's a number of CRAs around the city of Tampa. One is in downtown, and all downtown landowners have to put money into that fund, and then it goes towards improvements for the area. We stepped up with the help of some members of the City Council who were very pro-Tampa Theatre to put us in line to get that. We eventually did and now we were able to get fourteen million dollars over a four-year period. We've never had that kind of money before, ever. That was a huge game-changer for us. Getting an endowment in place is the next big challenge so that we're not living hand to mouth all the time.

I'd love to stay involved as long as they'll have me. It's something that I enjoy. When I was chairman, I brought a lot of people onto the board that I think have been really good additions. It's a working board. I represent mostly developers on real estate deals. I brought a number of those folks who I've worked with onto the board because they have a skill set that's useful, especially guys that have done a lot of historic work.

I think people are proud of Tampa Theatre. There's a lot of things that the city fathers shouldn't have done, like tear down that old courthouse. That was a great building. At least I think these people can be proud that they had the wisdom to not tear down Tampa Theatre.

Restoration

The board of directors voted in 1999 to add a restoration fee to ticket prices, twenty-five cents for movies and one dollar for concerts. At the time, it was estimated to generate $25,000 annually. The theater's increasing community support allowed for a quickening pace of restoration and upgrades. The cove lighting essential for making the atmospheric walls pop was brought back to life for the first time since the 1940s. The box office and entryway received an expert makeover and paint job by Jed Ellis. The theater restored the brilliant marquee and replaced the blade sign with a modern replica, together illuminated by more than two thousand lightbulbs. Presided over by Mayor Pam Iorio, a thousand well-wishers watched the ceremonial lighting of the new replica LED blade sign in 2004.

In 2006, the DIY Network show called *DIY to the Rescue* selected Tampa Theatre for an episode. Theater volunteer Catherine Sanders had contacted the television show after watching and wondering, "Why not us?" The show's crew taught a group of volunteers how to renovate the theater's dressing rooms and create a proper green room for performers. Beck Construction donated a quarter million dollars of labor and supplies to the project. Co-host Karil Champley said, "This is really special because of the building's history. We didn't want to build something [that] feels like a new addition."

Steady fundraising made the theater more capable of meeting crises head-on. In 2013, film distributors announced that they would be abandoning analog films in one year. For most commercial theaters, the news was of no consequence, as they were born digital, but one-third of the nation's theaters had not yet made the transition when the announcement was made. For older places with no money to go digital immediately, the announcement was a death sentence. The theater foundation was able to spend $150,000 to purchase a digital projector and sound system, giving *right top* The blade sign's replacement in 2004 was visible evidence of how far the scrappy community theater had come. Tampa Theatre.

right bottom Replacing a neon tube in 2023.Tampa Theatre.

Lighting up the new marquee in 2004. Tampa Theatre.

the venue a new lease on life. John Bell explained, "We are not going to alter the aesthetics of Tampa Theatre, but the technology used to present movies will need to evolve with whatever the industry is dictating."

Bell's stewardship of the theater amassed enough resources by 2017 to launch a series of updates and restoration projects that cost $6 million. Through dedicated fundraising and writing grants, the theater team had raised $4 million of the cost. Referred to as phase one, it represented the first half of the plan to prepare the palace for its second century. The aging facility and infrastructure required upgrades such as replacing the "Frankenstein-like switchboard" backstage with a modern electrical system and dimmers. Intense hurricane activity called for a new emergency generator in the event of power outages. The basement received new sump pumps and drainage.

A volunteer was responsible for a visit by *DIY to the Rescue* in 2006, when the show devoted an episode to fixing up one of Tampa Theatre's green rooms. Tampa Theatre.

bottom EverGreene Architectural Arts is a trusted partner in Tampa Theatre's restoration efforts. Tampa Theatre.

right Many of the statues needed care, with some wear in evidence. Tampa Theatre.

below Constant fundraising and restoration efforts ramped up in the 2000s. Here, the stripped-down lobby gets some attention. 2017. Tampa Theatre.

To raise money to replace the theater's seats, management held a "Cush Your Tush" campaign for better cushions and more legroom. Tampa Theatre.

Much of phase one went toward restoration efforts. Some changes made by the city over the years, such as the carpet, seat color, and interior paint, did not match Eberson's original vision. It had been Bell's long-sought goal to restore the theater's aesthetics to as close to the original as possible. With the care of a curator, Bell fretted over the details and weighed options for plasterwork, tapestries, and the lobby's exquisite multilayered paint, all signatures of John Eberson's aesthetic. Things like the pattern of the carpet and the color of the gargoyles required some serious research to get right. New carpet and drapes were matched with the originals and installed. Best of all for the comfort of patrons, phase one included new seating. The old seats had been installed nearly forty years before and served three million customers. The new seats featured more legroom than their predecessors, but the theater lost about two hundred seats in the process.

Once the new seating was in place, the theater leveraged it into a new fundraising campaign. Cheekily called "Cush Your Tush," the effort allowed patrons to "buy" a seat to be named after them, complete with a plaque on the back, for its working life. Given that the two previous sets of seats were in use for about fifty years each, it was safe to say that one's seat would welcome many tushes.

As part of the Cush Your Tush campaign to replace the theater's seating, the old seats were sold for use as home furnishings. Former house manager and longtime box office cashier Patt Vida styled hers in 2017. Courtesy of Patt Vida.

The Leases

John Bell had long been haunted not by ghosts, but another creeping menace, the leases for the land under Tampa Theatre. The palace had been built on shaky ground: two small parcels leased from three different owners. When the city rescued the theater from ruin, it inherited the leases and assumed the payments, one for the lobby and two for the auditorium, about $90,000 annually. It was understandably difficult for Bell and the theater's leadership to convince a succession of mayors to earmark scarce resources to buy the properties outright. But like a ticking bomb, the peaceful passing of time only deferred the crisis and could not be ignored forever.

Replacing the red chairs in 2017 made it possible to return to the auditorium's original color scheme. Architect John Eberson avoided red and gold, favoring soothing blue and earth tones. Tampa Theatre.

The lobby lease was paid to the Tampa Theatre Building Partnership, the group that had bought and rehabilitated the office tower attached to the theater in 1979. In 1998, the city entered negotiations to renew the lease.

Bell explained,

> The city renewed the lobby lease at the end of 1998, extending it for another twenty-five years, to make it sync up with the auditorium land lease. With the lobby time bomb solved for the time being, in the year 2000 I began to urge city officials to pursue full ownership of the theater property for preservation purposes. Every administration I dealt with did not seem to have an appetite to deal with it; they didn't feel any sense of urgency about resolving the leases. They could just kick it down the road to the next mayor. For us it wasn't just about preservation, it was also becoming a significant funding issue. With a cloud over the ownership of Theatre's real estate, we were blocked from even applying for funding for the Theatre's restoration work from many agencies and foundations. I felt like we were trying to run a race with our shoelaces tied together.
>
> We purposely recruited some savvy real estate minds [Bob Glaser and Steve Kelly] to serve on the board of Tampa Theatre to help us find solutions. It was exceedingly difficult to establish a value to buy out this land lease. In real estate, you usually look for comps [comparable real estate sales]. There were no comps since it was so unique. Another complicating factor was the language of the land lease, which specified that at the end of the lease term, any leasehold improvements on the land would become the landowner's property. So, if the land leases were allowed to expire, the city would no longer own the auditorium.

After Bob Glaser, CEO of Smith and Associates Realtors, joined the theater board in 2001, John Bell could rely on his wise counsel. Bell enthused to the press, "Bob not only understands real estate inherently, he understands how important it is. He has taken it as an almost personal mission." In 2005, with Glaser's help, the theater bought out one of the two owners of the auditorium lease for $200,000.

Bell said,

> It was a smooth transaction, one that came with a nice surprise. At closing we realized we weren't buying one half of the plot of land under the auditorium.

In 2009, theater president John Bell was pleased to buy out one of the leases on the building. Communications director Tara Schroeder bears witness. Tampa Theatre.

> We were buying an undivided interest in the entire parcel of land. That was good for us, since it gave us 50 percent ownership stake in the entire parcel. While we still couldn't do anything with our newfound ownership, for the first time we had some leverage with respect to the other half.

In 2009, the city refinanced some bonds and bought the lobby for $2 million. The purchase included a small retail space that would become the Taylor Screening Room. Mayor Pam Iorio appropriated the money amid painful cuts of $50 million from a budget dragged down by a deep recession. The theater then deeded the property to the city. In the process of buying out the lease, the city saved $1.5 million in future payments. Had negotiations failed, the theater would have been forced to vacate the lobby and improvise a new entrance.

Only one lease remained, but the owners would not budge from their vastly inflated asking price. Bell brought in another specialist to sit on the board and look into the problem. With his lifelong connection to Tampa Theatre, real estate attorney Jeff Shear joined the board in 2013 ready for a challenge. Shear said,

> The family that owned the other half was completely unreasonable. I thought that I would take a shot one more time. I went and tried to talk with these folks, thought that we could maybe meet in the middle somewhere. I had approached the previous mayor, Bob Buckhorn's administration, and said, "Look, we think the only way to get this done is for the city to condemn the land, the property." They had no interest in doing that because that would cost money, but that was really the only way to make them be reasonable. We think it's worth a couple hundred thousand dollars. We need to get it in front of a judge to really say, "All right, this is what it's worth," and to get this thing over with once and for all.
>
> When Mayor Jane Castor came in, I happened to have a relationship with the city attorney at that time and, and talked to her about it and said, "We've got to get the city to condemn this thing. Do it in eminent domain. That's the only way we're gonna get it." And time was continuing to tick. The city filed a condemnation lawsuit against the family and, as we expected, we settled it before court. We met somewhere in the middle a lot closer to our number.

That number was about $700,000 to $800,000. Bell said eminent domain brought the deal to closure.

> That family actually welcomed the eminent domain proceedings. They really didn't talk to each other. They recognized it was the only way that they could get it resolved. The deadline for when that lease expired was February 1, 2023, because that lease was executed in 1924, as they assembled the land. It was resolved in late 2022, about four months in advance of the expiration date.

Shear said, "That was a big accomplishment. I'm proud that we were able to make that happen while I was chairman. In theory they could have shut down the theater. Mayor Castor had the wisdom to understand that. Politically, having the theater shut down was a nonstarter."

Bell said, "When it was resolved, it opened up certain big grants at the State

Tampa Theatre purchased a neighboring retail space in 2009 as part of a daring plan. Tampa Theatre.

of Florida we could not get because there was this cloud over the real estate. The Tampa Theatre, minus the privately owned office condos above the lobby, is now owned free and clear by the City of Tampa."

The Second Screen

The most daring part of the phase one plan involved acquiring a second screen for Tampa Theatre. In 2019, the board voted to take over the flower shop next door and convert it into a small theater.

The commitment of the theater's board members is exemplified by John T. Taylor, whose support made the new mini theater possible. He grew up in West Lafayette, Indiana, and worked hard managing livestock on his father's large farm. Taylor's love for athletics was only rivaled by his love for popcorn and cinema at the Arc Theatre there. "You could see Roy Rogers and Gene Autry," he said. "That's the way I grew up." After service in the Air Force and a career of managing the family farm, he sold the estate and wandered a while.

In retirement, Taylor eventually landed on Davis Islands in 1996, where he found Tampa Theatre as his new connection for classic cinema and adventurous programming. For Taylor, helping the theater was a natural impulse, given his passion for charity and love of cinema. It was Taylor who suggested breaking up John Bell's ambitious restoration plans into distinct phases for fundraising purposes. He also helped establish a relationship between the theater and the Tampa Club, a group of the area's top businesspeople.

After serving on the theater's board for six years, Taylor donated $500,000 to Tampa Theatre in 2018. He explained,

> My whole philosophy has been giving back for all the good things that I've had in my life. I served in the Air Force because I thought that I should do that. I was a city councilman. And I have always tried to do things to help charities. John, Tara, and Jill were all interested in having a small theater. It was fortunate that they were in a position with the flower shop right next door. They needed something to kickstart that whole thing.

The John T. Taylor Screening Room's opening in 2024. *From left,* Tampa Theatre board chair Mike Hooker, Tampa Mayor Jane Castor, John Bell, City Councilwoman Gwen Henderson, and benefactor John T. Taylor. Tampa Theatre.

The Tampa Theatre team in the John T. Taylor Screening Room, affectionately known as T2, in 2024. *Bottom row (from left):* Leah LoSchiavo Doan, Joey Hager, Kelly Enman, John Bell, Devin Dominguez, Jacob Otto, Shana Nichols. *Middle row:* Kim Stewart, Sydney Grogan, Jill Witecki, James DeFord, Léa Van Name, Dawn Kidle. *Top row:* Derek Bartenfelder, Kevin Lowther, Spot LaRussa, Lloyd Pearson, Adi Sudhakaran, Cathy Prance. Tampa Theatre.

The new micro theater opens up a range of programming possibilities. Tampa Theatre.

Taylor's donation galvanized the effort to fulfill the board's $2.9 million dream of a second screen, with funding completed by Hillsborough County and Tampa's Community Redevelopment Agency. The John T. Taylor Screening Room, also known as T2, greatly broadened the palette of the theater's programmers. Although a new theater with forty-three seats does not sound like a major addition, it was a game-changer. Most film distributors demand that current first-run films be screened a certain number of times to be eligible for any given venue. With only one screen and stage, it could be very difficult if not impossible to show a film every day for a week at Tampa Theatre. The Taylor room and its screen gave the theater much more flexibility to show a film there while the main auditorium hosted a live event or another film.

Opened in June 2024, the John T. Taylor Screening Room is a fabulous self-contained theater with its own street entrance, bar, and restroom. Its tasteful design and decor evoke Eberson's style without trying to imitate it. The premium sound system from Boston Light and Sound is not to be missed.

6

The Hero's Journey

Words such as "director" or "artist" seem to be inadequate descriptions for Brett Culp. Although he has described himself as a filmmaker and social entrepreneur, that falls short, too. Culp's story, in which Tampa Theatre plays an important role, reveals his contagious enthusiasm, deep well of inspiration, and voice as a storyteller. Culp talked about his background.

> My family's been in Tampa for five generations. Tampa is a very special place for us. I've had many different careers over the years. One of them is documentary filmmaker. I've made three films; all have premiered here at Tampa Theatre.
>
> My real first memory of Tampa Theatre was in 1989 when the movie *Batman* came out by Tim Burton. Some genius of programming here decided to play the old Batman serials from the 1930s. I was so fascinated by that. I begged my mom to bring me here. I remember sitting in the theater, it wasn't very crowded, it was on a Saturday matinee screening. When I walked in the door, I learned the age and history of the theater. It occurred to me at twelve years old, as I'm sitting there, I am watching this Batman serial in the exact same space where my great-grandfather might have been, watching this exact same serial way back when.
>
> I didn't have words for it then, but I can say it this way now, that as a lifelong lover of cinema and movies, I was part of something sacred, something that transcended movies. You can walk into any box room theater in any town in the world and watch any movie on a big screen. But when you can watch the movie in the space where your ancestors watched it, when you can watch *Casablanca* or *The Wizard of Oz* and know that people who are long dead had their first experience with this movie in the exact same immaculate beautiful space you're sitting in now, looking up at that same sky, there's something al-

The intricate details of Eberson's atmospherics reflect a bygone era of theater construction. 2025. Courtesy of Jeff Fay.

most primal. As a lover of stories and cinema, I feel that way every time I watch a movie in this space, particularly historic movies.

When I was in college, I started making wedding videos so I could quit my job at Target. Whenever a [Tampa Bay] Buccaneer [football player] got married, I filmed their wedding. I traveled all over the world doing that. I developed all these skills, equipment, and resources. I realized that I had dreams, I had unique stories I wanted to tell. I was looking for a way to talk about the power of stories that was very relatable.

I'm a lifelong superhero fan. I love Batman. I had the idea, "What if we use Batman, this character that's been around for so many decades, that's evolved, that's had so many different versions?" The first documentary I made was called *Legends of the Knight,* and it was about stories of people who had been inspired by Batman to be better people. At a deeper level, the film was about the power of storytelling. The stories that we interact with affect the way we see ourselves and who we can be in the world. I didn't realize it, but I was tapping into a very deep zeitgeist of cultural energy about that topic that had not been tapped into before. It went viral.

Many filmmakers in the region have chosen Tampa Theatre as the location of their premieres. For Brett Culp, screening his first film, *Legends of the Knight,* in 2013 was a dream come true. Courtesy of Brett Culp.

Culp soon decided on his film's first showing.

When we finished *Legends of the Knight,* the only thing I knew was that I wanted to premiere here at Tampa Theatre. Once I knew that, I said, "Whatever revenue comes in from that screening, I want to give it to Metropolitan Ministries," which is a local charity our family has been involved in for a long time. I knew that if I could do that I would have succeeded, that I would have had my moment for me to be there with my family, with my kids, with my parents.

Before the premiere, we had a little pre-party at the Columbia Restaurant in one of those little dining rooms. My dad gave a speech that night and he said, "Son, you've done lots of great things in your life. But this kind of work,

left *Black Panther* inspired some serious superhero cosplay in 2018. Tampa Theatre.

below Heroes and villains often share the spotlight. Longtime concession lead Calvin Mynatt (*left*) and T. J. McDonnell attend a screening of *Batman* (1989) in 2024. Tampa Theatre.

> this kind of storytelling, is really what you were made to do." I remember having a validating experience with multiple generations of my family, sitting in that room at the Columbia, and then us driving over here to the Tampa Theatre.

When they arrived, they had a surprise, Culp said.

> Somebody on the team figured out how to put the bat signal up in the sky inside the theater. They didn't even tell me they were going to do that until it was done, and I walk in and I look up and I'm like, "Perfect, this is just perfect." It was transcendent in a way that I couldn't capture, it only could be experienced. I will never forget that feeling of walking in, and having people watch my documentary under this beautiful starlit sky that I loved, with the bat signal up there. I remember having a standing ovation at the end of that premiere. There was something in me that was dancing with five generations of my family in this space, being who I was created to be, doing what I was created to do.

The experience left an impression on Culp.

> I remember waking up the next morning, and I said, "I want everyone in the world to have the opportunity to feel the way I feel right now. Having this incredible experience of premiering this film, with all my friends and family, raising money for a local charity. This is amazing." We created an alliance with a theatrical distributor that allowed anyone in the world to request a screening of that film in their local movie theater, with the proceeds from that screening going to whatever local charity they chose. This phenomenon of Batman fans took over. People all over the world started requesting these screenings, a hundred and ten cities, and raised over $100,000.
>
> I have no doubt that in my unconscious mind, that my experience on that first night here at Tampa Theatre, all of that played into this idea that a movie has to be more than a movie. For me, when *Legends of the Knight* premiered on Netflix, that was awesome. But the premiere here at Tampa Theatre was better. Having those shared experiences, we did share something together that becomes part of the history of this space forever. As human beings, we all want to feel that our spirit, at the depth of our soul, that we belong somewhere. It is a beautiful thing as an artist to feel that your work belongs somewhere. My films belong here.

Peeling Back the Layers

Jeff Greene's painting career ranged from portraits to massive murals before he founded EverGreene Architectural Arts Company in 1978. The specialty contractor is among the very best in the world at restoration and fine interior work. To restore John Eberson's exquisite paint and decor, there are none better than EverGreene. Their forensic work on the box office and lobby helped crack the code for the rest of the theater's restoration.

Greene explained his company's work on Tampa Theatre.

> Starting in the mid-eighties, we got involved in preservation and interior decoration. When we did our first theater in '88, I fell in love with the architecture. I think I've worked on four hundred to date. I think we've worked on more Eberson theaters than anybody else that's living.

Jeff Greene (*right*), founder of EverGreene Architectural Arts, with John Bell (*left*). Greene is one of the country's leading experts in the restoration of historic buildings and was personally involved in EverGreene's restoration of the Tampa Theatre lobby in 2017. Tampa Theatre.

I would say that the Tampa is probably the most extant Eberson existing. It's more intact than any other Ebersons that I'm aware of. I'm familiar with all of them, and it's magnificent. It's really extraordinary because it has all the furnishings, the paintings, the tapestries, the plaster hasn't been mucked about, nobody's poked holes in it, nobody's changed anything. It didn't go into ruin, was never abandoned. It was never turned into a porno theater. It's a smaller theater, much more intimate, which is actually part of its charm. I think that's why people love it, because of its scale. It's a very personable place.

One of the difficult things in the lobby was the Vitrolite glass. They don't make it any more. We found just enough to match the colors for downstairs. The statues had broken fingers. We had a very talented woman rebuild all the statues with broken parts that had been damaged over the years.

The Michel Angelo art studios produced the plaster. Oftentimes you'll find the same statues, and the same plaster ornament was used over and over again. He'd cast smooth ornament plaster, and then they would texture everything with a coating, this little pebble texture. He would stain the plaster to a kind of earth tone with glazes, and then he would begin to polychrome in these vibrant, chromatic colors. That's Eberson's signature decorating style of the period. He almost never used metallic paint, which was interesting because in most of these movie palaces, they made them sparkle by putting a lot of gold, aluminum, silver, and everything else.

To examine the layers of color, Greene said,

You make exposure windows, so you're literally stripping back layers of paint to try to reveal the original. In the process of removing layers, you can't really visually see what it looked like. To get the true color, you take a little chip, and

John Eberson's paint work is intricate and difficult to replicate. Jed Ellis used forensic techniques to reveal how the color looked a century ago. 2017, Jeff Fay.

you put it in a cross section under the microscope, and then you match the color under balanced lighting.

In the lobby, we looked at the microscope and got the chroma chronologies. You try to understand, how was he using these colors to try to express something? Where did he use warm colors on the highlights? Where did they use cool colors in the interstices? Was he trying to make certain things come forward and go back? Where did he use contrast? You kind of have to crawl into his mind. There was a formula, there was a system. Once you understand the grammar of that language that he's using, then you can speak articulately in that syntax.

Eberson thought of it as this kind of gestalt, the whole thing altogether, the carpet, the drapery, the seat covers. There's always little clues that help you with the overall color palette, find a piece of an original fabric, or you pull back a tapestry, and you see all the original colors. You find a piece of tile, you find a piece of carpet underneath the seat, every little thing gives

> you a clue to how all the pieces fit together so that you haven't disturbed the memory of the place.

Beyond forensic techniques, Greene explained, artistic sensitivity was employed in replicating the details and overall effects.

> There's another element besides the forensics and doing the research and getting all the specifics right, there's also a little bit of artistry. Does it feel right? "Authenticity" is the word that comes to mind, but it's sort of ironic because the whole flow is a put-on, right? It's a show. The day it opened, it looked like it had been there for a long time. Even though it was fresh and new, it already looked distressed and had this patina on it. It's the best Eberson there is. It's not the biggest but it's the best.

The Curator

After spending more than forty years working in the theater, President John Bell was still discovering new details about the atmospheric palace and its history. Bell takes a curator's pride and fan's delight in every detail, enthralled by the artistry of John Eberson, Tampa Theatre's "atmospheric" architect. Bell said he continued noticing touches.

> My favorite details may be whatever catches my eye that day. There's just so much going on that it's difficult to really think you've seen all of it. I was here about fifteen years before I noticed a particular detail. In the lower men's lounge, there were these weird sconces, they were asymmetrical, and they just sort of had a bulb on one end. Then I saw an old historic photograph where the sign for the men's room said "smoking parlor" because you could smoke in the building. When I went in there again, I noticed that those asymmetrical sconces were pipes. They were smoking pipes, and the lightbulb was screwed into the bowl of the pipe. I'd never picked up on that before. You can walk through this building a hundred times, a thousand times, and you'll see something different. When the carpet was restored in 2017 to the original pattern, that may be one of my favorite elements. When we had a solid carpet before, it was okay. But when you saw the original design go down, then it was like, "Oh, well, yeah, this all makes sense now."

Restoration work has breathed new life into the old building. Details like these gargoyles are meant to look the same as on opening day. 2017, Jeff Fay.

Some details, like the intercom system with old telephone fixtures, are kept in their antique condition. Tampa Theatre.

One favorite feature attracts attention, Bell said.

> I love the gargoyles. When they visit for a field trip, the children love gargoyles too. It's usually pretty early in the morning, they will come in and see the gargoyles in the lobby, then one of them will go "Oooh." Then pretty soon you have five hundred children going "Oooh" because they are attention-getters. The restoration work that was done on them revealed that they were far more three-dimensional than we had first imagined. They had been painted out over the years in some sort of stone-gray thing. When the restoration on them was done, we realized that these guys have abs, they've been working out. They are really fit gargoyles. They are one of the defining features of the building. I had an architectural historian once tell me that when a gargoyle is on the inside of the building, it's not a gargoyle, it's called a grotesque. I thought that was pretty harsh. We're still gonna call them gargoyles.

Bell pointed out natural features in the motifs as well.

> We have birds throughout the building and flowering vines and trees—it's a garden, a Mediterranean courtyard. In the lobby, there were two stuffed

macaws that had deteriorated over time. Years ago, we had to get new ones to replace them. We thought, "We'll just get two more macaws. How hard can this be?" And then we realized it's hard because macaws live a long time, like seventy-five, eighty years? We put the word out to like Busch Gardens and the San Diego Zoo and all these other places like, "Put us on your wait list. We'd like first dibs." The word had gotten out, six months go by, and we finally got a call from a dead-bird dealer in New York. And he said, "Hey I understand you're looking for a couple macaws?" And I said, "Yeah." He said, "I got a couple macaws for you." I didn't ask any questions. We paid the man, we got them, and we installed them.

I tell that story on tours because it points to our philosophy of restoration here, that we want everything to be authentic. I could have had a ton of fun if I'd gone to Michaels craft store and gotten some Styrofoam and a glue gun and some fake feathers and built me a macaw, but it wouldn't be authentic. In the public spaces of this building, everything that we do is going to be painstakingly authentic. If there were real macaws there, we're gonna put real ones back. If it was a walnut handrail, walnut is going back. We're not going to substitute a cheaper type of wood. One of the reasons that the theater became endangered was that, economically, it doesn't make sense. That's why we're nonprofit. It's got so many competitive disadvantages. But the one advantage that we have over every other venue is that we are the authentic historic theater. That's what we lean into 100 percent, because that's our advantage.

The macaws hanging in the lobby are an example of John Bell's philosophy to strive for authenticity when restoring original elements of the theater Tampa Theatre.

Authenticity sets Tampa Theatre apart, Bell said.

The theater is like a museum and an operating theater all rolled into one. And that's both the joy and the challenge too because it's got to operate. We don't throw anything out. That's both good and bad because we don't have anyplace to put stuff. If something original breaks, we don't toss it, we put it in a closet somewhere. We wait until we can restore it and put it back out. The music stands, the old intercom system that does not work

It took many years before Bell noticed that the light fixtures in the smoking room are shaped like tobacco pipes. Tampa Theatre.

> anymore, we're going to restore it for its looks, all of those things are important. It's part of the fabric of the theater.

Tampa Theatre is unique in that sense even among Eberson theaters, Bell said.

> The other Eberson atmospherics that I've had the pleasure of visiting, they're all wonderful, but none of them have the original furnishings that we have. I remember walking through an Eberson atmospheric that had been restored, and it was beautiful, but I was walking through with some staff members from the Tampa Theatre and I kept whispering to them, "What's missing? There's something missing." Then it dawned on me that it's the furnishings. The tables, the lamps, the chairs, the mirrors, all of those original pieces, which are still here. We are by far the most complete, intact Eberson atmospheric in the world. That says something about prior management; it says something about the city's foresight to save it immediately instead of letting it languish for years. We're very fortunate to have all of that.

Like others, though, the theater is well built, Bell said.

> It's a very strong building. There is a story about one of John Eberson's theaters in the 1950s that was torn down. The Paradise in Chicago was a big monster of a theater. The general contractor for the demolition company thought, "It'll take me four months to knock this thing down." So, they bid on it based on that. They did not realize that a one-foot column in the blueprints was actually three feet. It took that company eighteen months of trying to knock it down, and they couldn't. That company went out of business and went bankrupt. I believe the owner committed suicide, and then it took an-

other company another six months to complete the demolition. So, the lesson is, don't tear down a John Eberson theater. One, because you can't, and number two, because you shouldn't.

Bell remarked on his own professional life at Tampa Theatre.

I never mapped out a life career. I just go to work every day and do the best I can. After about ten years, I realized this is not a bad place to be at all. I've certainly had other offers and opportunities, but I've never been interested simply because it's such a spectacular building to walk into every day and the community dearly loves it.

The Scribe

For Leah LoSchiavo Doan, working for Tampa Theatre has been a lifelong relationship that has deepened over time. From the stage and concession counter to the office upstairs, Doan has worked her way through the palace to become operations executive assistant.

Doan recalled,

I was born and raised in Tampa. I started going to the theater as a child. My mother would take me there on field trips. My first memory of being there was when I was four, and I think we went to see *Gaslight* with Ingrid Bergman because I remember walking down one of the staircases of the very back of the theater and seeing one of the standing lamps at the foot of the stairwell and thinking that's what a gas light was because I had no context of what was really happening in the film.

Later on that year, we went for a Christmas program. We were walking through the doors between the auditorium and the lobby, and there was a manager trying to get a kid on stage to do a drawing for a Christmas tree. I raised my hand. I have that memory of being four years old and standing on the stage of Tampa Theatre gazing out at the audience. A drawing for a Christmas tree. I was the person who pulled the ticket out that announced the winner. I remember feeling very small and very scared but also very awed by the experience. I participated in the school field trip programs as a child.

From left, Leah LoSchiavo Doan, Callie Lawson, and Georgeanne Crabtree breaking character at the first WineFest event, "Gone with the Wine," in 2002. Tampa Theatre.

Growing up, Doan became fixated on theater as an art form. A love for Tampa Theatre seemed to be a natural outgrowth of her newfound interest in the arts. While she was working a series of jobs with a friend, they ended up working at Tampa Theatre in 1997. Doan described her first jobs there.

I started tearing tickets and shuffling popcorn and working in the concessions stand. I had a personal goal of having sold out the theater. We did have a screening of *Gone with the Wind* in one of our summer classics, and we sold it out. I sold it on five-dollar roll tickets in an hour. Just by myself. *The Blair Witch Project* [1999] was a big deal when we showed that. We sold out the entire opening weekend, and I think over eight screenings we had something like eleven thousand people come through. From there I started working in the box office during the daytime. Still in college, I was [majoring] in theater performance at TheatreUSF, [while] working day box [office] and learning, almost apprentice style, how the business functions. The day box has all of the transactions of the theater. Everything goes through that cell in the daily reports.

From '97 to about 2001 I was primarily part time, and I didn't become full-time staff until after that. I moved up to the administrative office, kind of as an office manager, and additional box office support but on the administrative side as opposed to the direct sales point side. By the time I left, my title was operations supervisor. I was handling files and contracts, website and membership, recordkeeping, doing time cards. I used to take the minutes at board meetings; I supported executive positions and development positions. I felt very well rounded in what I learned about the business and venue operation.

After graduation in 2000, she worked as an actor with Jobsite Theater and American Stage in St. Petersburg. Doan said those roles dovetailed with her theater job.

It was very convenient to be doing theater and have my day job. The job wasn't like a management position. I was primarily an assistant. I wasn't necessarily managing other people. I could come in, do my job, and then have this whole other life beyond that. Not the case today. There's a lot more thought, planning, and strategy now.

I had such a solid skill set administratively in a very unique industry. That meant a lot to me. I was able to transfer that into multiple other positions including working for another historic theater in California. I worked in insurance in New York for the brief period of time that I lived there, and I just could not wrap my head around what I was doing to support that organization that basically sold insurance administration to larger companies. I could be shown how to do pivot tables and spreadsheets, but I struggled and didn't feel at home. Whereas at Tampa Theatre, the relationship I have with the people there and the building inspires me to learn whatever I need to learn to keep the place supported, functioning, and flourishing.

When I decided to leave Tampa in 2010, I had planned to move and be out of Florida permanently. The pandemic changed that for the better. I'm very happy to have come back in 2020. I do feel very fortunate that I get to work at Tampa Theatre, and I'm very passionate about the work that I do. The things that I've done in service of nonprofit cultural arts institutions I can't imagine myself doing anywhere else. I would not do finance anywhere else. I would not do HR [human resources] anywhere else, like for a tech company or a hedge fund company or hospital. I'm driven by my passion for the theater.

Charlie Chaplin made a special appearance at Oscar Night 2001, posing here with Jim Porter (*center*) and Carolyn Heller (*right*). Vice president and director of operations Cathy Prance arranged for the celebrity's appearance. Tampa Theatre.

Doan described her personal connection to Tampa Theatre.

> When I started going it felt it was an extension of my home. It's where I live. It was just there for me and my family and my friends, and it eventually became my career. That feeling of belonging to it and how it belonged to me from four years old. I've cleaned every inch of that place. I know the dressing rooms; I know the green room; I know the catwalks; I know every nook and cranny. Being in there without an audience is its own experience, just walking through it every day when the lights are out. I knew how to turn everything on and run everything on the old electric board. When you first engage with the theater, you're just overwhelmed by how stunning it is. When you become a steward of the building it's like, oh, I really wish we could get that thing repaired today.

Operations manager Joey Hager made it a mission to reconstruct the theater's first century of programming. Tampa Theatre.

The Archivist

Joey Hager grew up across Tampa Bay in Clearwater and developed a keen interest in cinema and classic films through frequent trips to Clearwater's Capitol Theatre. He moved to Tampa to study English and creative writing. When he needed funds to help get him through college, a job at a multiplex theater made sense. He quickly worked his way up the ranks and managed a location for five of the seven years he spent there.

Hager recounted his early experiences at Tampa Theatre that led to his working there.

> When I finally moved to Tampa, finding Tampa Theatre was like, "Okay, good. There's another theater in my backyard that I'll be able to enjoy." The first time I came here was for a community screening of *Dead Poets Society* right after Robin Williams passed away. I remember dragging some friends, parked on the street, turned the corner, saw the blade sign, and that was it. I knew that I had found it. We always sat in the balcony at the Capitol. So, I immediately went right up to the mezzanine, came up those stairs, saw the Venus, saw the stars, and it was immediate. Just the most beautiful place I've ever been in in my life. That would have been the end of summer 2014.
>
> I was very experienced at my [multiplex] job. I was one of the most tenured managers in a market with quite a lot of turnover. It had never occurred to me in all those years that I could work here at Tampa Theatre. Despite all that experience, I still felt like I was standing on the corner holding a baseball and this was the World Series. Until the position I'm in now opened up and I looked at the job description. I was like, "This is the moment. I have to go for it."

When Hager was hired as operations manager in 2023, he felt confident enough in his job running the ticketing system that he could afford to be curious. The newcomer quickly found the collection of old files and other materials in the office compiled by Tara Schroeder and Janna Jones. With his passion for film programming and classic cinema, Hager immediately set to the task of reconstructing the history of every film shown at Tampa Theatre.

> In my interview, we talked about the upcoming hundredth anniversary, so that was already kind of kicking around in my brain. That is a really big moment, not only for Tampa Theatre but also that moment in film history. I wanted to know, just personally, every film that played here and by extension every film that had never played here. I got here, and I suggested, "Is there a record? Is there a history of all the films?" And everyone laughed, "Of course not." I brought it up that I wanted to do that.
>
> That was kind of my first big green flag here because what I was asking to do was a leisure project. It wasn't about efficiency. It wasn't about saving us money. It wasn't about really making Tampa Theatre a better-operated place, it was for fun. It was for us. They could have very easily been like, "That

doesn't really do much for us." But they were over the moon, very excited, like, "Yes, that would be a great tool for us to have." I kind of framed it as a very dynamic tool for the future of film programming here.

Hager's enjoyment in cataloging Tampa Theatre's film showings is evident in his description:

> The first time that Dorothy opens the door and the Technicolor pops [in *The Wizard of Oz*], the first time that anyone in Tampa saw that happen was in this building. First time that the camera dollies in, unveils [actor Bela] Lugosi's face in *Dracula,* our proscenium framed that. Those things happened here. That's kind of fueled this archival interest for me, trying to identify as many of those moments as I can. If we know what our first century looked like, we can lay a good foundation for what we want to accomplish in terms of programming in the second century. Are there films that we've missed? Would we like those films to become part of our story? Are there films that played in that first century that haven't played since that we would like to reintroduce to our community? Selecting those experiences for people to have and remember is a very important job, a very sacred job, especially for a community so large and diverse.

The Advocate

In 2012, Jill Witecki took a job as Tampa Theatre's director of marketing and community relations. The work came naturally to her; aside from being a seasoned public relations manager, she had been an advocate of Tampa Theatre for most of her life.

Witecki recalled her introduction to the theater.

> I was taking French in high school and there was a field trip here at Tampa Theatre for French Culture Day. There was an afternoon of programming, a live ballet presentation, and a French film. My mom was a chaperone. We all came down here to go to lunch at CDB's [Italian restaurant] across the street and then go to this presentation at Tampa Theatre. I was a transplant; I didn't get down here until junior high. I had not had the grade school field trips that a lot of my classmates had. They had already seen Tampa Theatre, but it was

new for me. I remember the orchestra level where we were sitting. I was falling in love right there.

Whatever the film was, I couldn't tell you the title, I'm sure it was approved by the county. I remember that it was by far the raunchiest thing that any of us had ever seen in a school setting. It was kind of a romp, a farce. For example, there was a scene where one of the women was getting a bikini wax, and it was tastefully shot, but it was clear what was happening. My poor mother was sitting there in this group of students, trying to cover the eyes of the kids sitting around her, probably ninth or tenth grade. I mean, certainly this was not the worst thing that any of us had ever seen, it was just the fact that it was a school-sanctioned field trip.

For communications director Jill Witecki, one of the benefits of working and playing at Tampa Theatre is "that feeling of belonging to it and how it belongs to me." Tampa Theatre.

The French movie was silly and nobody cared about the ballet, but walking into this building [was impressive] for me. That whole day of this amazing building and drinking cappuccinos across the street with lunch at CDB's. It was such a weird mush of emotions of being very grown up and coming to the theater downtown and then going and having coffee. But also having this experience with my mom of finding this really cool place in a city that we had moved to a couple of years before.

I grew up in St. Louis, and Tampa was so different. I was not a kid inclined or immediately able to fit in. I was still trying to kind of find myself and figure out what being a teenager was without my support network of friends that I had grown up with. Finding this place it was like, this is something cool, something that I'm going to be able to show to other people. I can advocate for this place and bring other people here and hope some of the cool of Tampa Theatre rubs off on me. My friends and I came here a lot.

As a self-described "arts dork" Witecki dreamed of writing for an entertainment magazine or being a film critic for a newspaper. After graduating from the University of Missouri in 1999, she took a clerk position to get her foot in the door at the *Tampa Tribune.* She leveraged her talents to become a features writer as the old paper faced extinction. Jumping to public relations, she mastered the role at Busch

Gardens, dealing with everything from the announcement of new rides to the death of one of their wild animals.

All the while, Witecki had become deeply involved in Tampa Theatre during her spare time. She attended Tara Schroeder's "Theaterology" course so she could give tours as a volunteer docent. She joined the Balcony Club, a popular group devoted to the palace's preservation, and served on the WineFest committee for several years. When Schroeder had to leave in 2012, she warned Witecki that the position was very demanding. With so much love for the theater and so few resources for so long, Schroeder found it difficult to say no to taking on new projects. Over the years, she added more functions and programs to her schedule until she was burnt out. Witecki applied for the position and was immediately put at ease by John Bell's assurance that her hiring was an opportunity to hone down the role to its essentials and assign additional tasks to others. After some initial anxiety, Witecki soon recognized that she was in the right place at the right time as downtown Tampa reawakened around the theater. She recalled,

> The budget was very focused, let's say. There wasn't a ton of money in marketing, and it made it very easy to kind of focus on the basics. The organization has grown a lot since then. The programming has grown a lot since then. The marketing job is really just trying to figure out how to constantly remind people that we're here, here's what we're doing. If you're not interested in the thing we're doing this weekend that's okay, you might be interested in the thing that's happening next weekend. Tampa has changed a lot in twelve years, most of it for the better. The event calendar of entertainment options in Tampa and the surrounding areas is getting denser.
>
> For twelve years, I've said, "If I have to bring people into the theater one at a time, that is so much more cost-effective than running a bunch of advertisements." That person who's standing out on the sidewalk looking at our poster, and when you start talking to them, they're like, "Oh, yeah, we just moved to town, and what is this place? What do you all do here?" Come inside, let me show you, give me ten minutes to tell you the history. That's far better time and money spent than another newspaper ad.

The theater's charm keeps people coming back, Witecki said.

No detail was too small for architect John Eberson. This "Tot's Pot" in the ladies' room is available for young ladies. Tampa Theatre.

A lot of people's stories about coming to Tampa Theatre started as a kid or with a parent or with a grandparent. It's always been part of their life, or it's something that was kind of handed down to them from another generation. There's magic here. People are passionate about this building in a way that they aren't about any other.

There is something about this building that when people walk in, they are completely drawn to it and the energy here. I've had people that have walked into the building for the first time and sat down on the floor or walked in and said, "I feel like I could live here. I wish I could spend the night here." Would you ever walk into an AMC and sit down on the floor? No, that's gross. You would be stuck there forever. We have some beautiful historic buildings. Would you ever walk into City Hall and say, "Man, I'd really like to spend the night here"? There's just something different about the energy here that is warm and welcoming and positive and makes people feel like home when they walk in. A lot of that is the people who work here and the warm welcome that we're able to give people. But I think there's something in the building that creates that positive energy, and once you felt it once, you want to come back and feel again.

Speaking of her own family, Witecki said,

My girls feel like they own the place. The little toilet in the bathroom is just for them. Their first trips to Tampa Theatre were as newborns. I have changed diapers on the stoop outside the light board. They have been through every inch of this building, as has my dog. My dog has run the aisles of this building over and over again. There's not a lot of places that are that supportive of work-life balance. I tell people that all the time, that working at Tampa Theatre is like family, we love like family, we fight like family. Everybody's in it for the same reason, the good of the organization, the good of the theater.

The Maestro

As a postdoctoral student at the University of Michigan, Steven Ball's lifelong obsession with the theater organ led him to Tampa Theatre. When veteran organist Rosa Rio came onto the scene, Tara Schroeder contacted Ball, who was at the University of Michigan at the time, to visit and meet her. For him, the meeting's effect was as electrifying as Rio's first encounter with the theater's Wurlitzer.

Ball recalled Rio's importance to his own work.

I was very interested in giving theater the appropriate recognition it deserves as an American dialect of the organ. It had been taken for granted or maligned over the years. My interest was in trying to find primary source material to bolster my argument that this is a legitimate art form. To perform well on the instrument is just as difficult as performing a legitimate piece of classical organ music by Bach or Max Reger or any of the other composers that are taken seriously.

As Tampa Theatre's artist in residence, Steven Ball is a one-man orchestra who accompanies silent films on the Mighty Wurlitzer organ. Tampa Theatre.

On occasion, other musicians join in the fun. This screening of Buster Keaton's *The General* featured an orchestra. Tampa Theatre.

Rosa was what ultimately brought me here. She was terribly important. She was the key to so much that I couldn't understand about the past. She was the living link that I was missing. You can read a lot in books but there's something that is beyond all of that. Art for me is when something is greater than the sum of its parts, and that's the gift she gave me. She became a friend.

The response to Rosa's playing was positively electric. I remember the show *Beyond the Rocks* she played for. That was a recently restored film I had never seen. I still remember where I sat up in the balcony. Every time I watch a film here, I find myself sitting in that same seat because that was the moment so many things changed. Rosa was the catalyst. That's a good way for me to describe her. You can have a chemical reaction with all the right ingredients in place but until the catalyst is there, the reaction doesn't happen. That was Rosa.

Maybe 20 percent of the scores for the silent movies survived. What you were getting in the early days was basically a couple of pages of suggestions. Play the "Heroic March" by somebody or other for two and a half minutes. Then play Beethoven "Adagio" for another three minutes. You get two or three pages of this. Rosa said, "Usually when these scores arrived, they were all junk, we'd just throw them out." She had a much more effective way of doing it herself. She did a lot of composing for films. I do as well. For me, the average silent film takes about forty hours to put together. You have to watch the film and study every movement of every character in every detail. What is the emotional intent? What is that character trying to convey? You have to know exactly the second when everything shifts emotionally in a film. Then you have to time it all to music.

Ball, who became Tampa Theatre's artist in residence, described playing live accompaniment for silent films and Rosa Rio's great talent at the theater's organ.

> You can't hear the dialogue, and you don't realize that your imagination is actually taking over. You're watching these characters have an exchange. You start to imagine the exchange that's happening. That element of the imagination is what makes silent film such a powerful experience. The speed of the audience reaction determines how quickly you can move to the next cue. I can't imagine anything I'd rather do than being able to tell the tale in that way.
>
> Rosa used to say that the reason why the organ console is here is because your job is to draw the audience into the film. If I do my job correctly, I completely disappear for them. The greatest compliment anyone could tell me is that I completely disappeared, that they totally forgot I was there. If I'm drawing their attention to the music, I'm doing the wrong thing. Rosa was fabulous about being in the spotlight. When she wanted the spotlight, she stole the show. But as a film player, she knew exactly when and how and where to direct the spotlight. Maybe that power is part of her magic.
>
> She was like the theater organ, immensely colorful, very showbiz. She liked bright sparkly things. Yet, very much in every way, a southern lady. She was this elegant, graceful lady who also had this wild side. She knew exactly when to play the wild card. She was in many ways like the instrument, quirky, colorful, and full of magic.

The theater itself enhances audiences' experiences, Ball said.

> The Tampa Theatre is one of the finest preserved movie palaces in the world. As a result of the unique constraints of the architecture here, it's very intimate and has exceptional acoustics. The audience can communicate to me. They

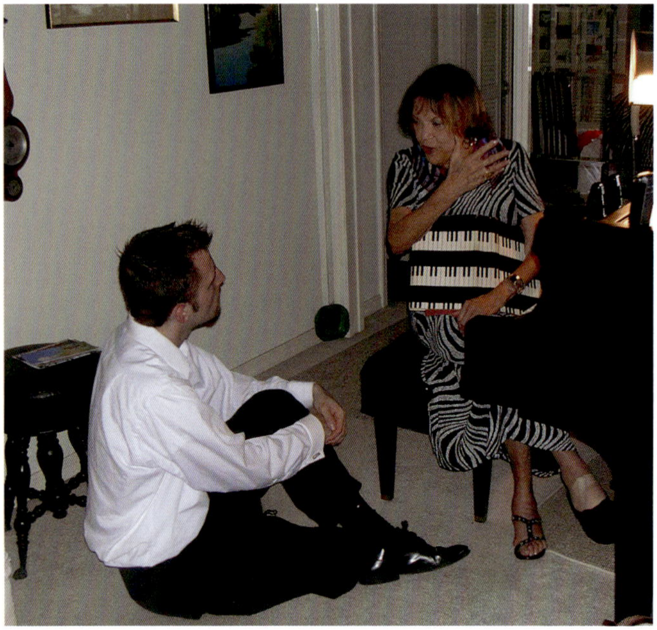

For Steven Ball, finding Tampa Theatre and Rosa Rio (age 103 in this photo) provided the kind of education most organists could only dream of. Steven Ball.

don't realize that they're doing it, but the acoustics here are truly exceptional. Visually, it's splendid. His [Eberson's] idea was that you would design a place that looked almost as if it had always been here. It just really looks like a piece of another time. So there's a unique magic here that even in Eberson buildings is extra-special here.

Tampa Theatre is a sort of an artifact. It's an artifact of this brief flash of silent picture history [in] the entertainment industry as it exploded and developed and then hit the Depression and evolved. What made the first hundred years special was not only the fact that the Tampa Theatre survived with such integrity but also in the way it is charting the course in how these buildings can be used. It's also reminding Americans of their cultural identity. There's something uniquely important here. There is a cultural patrimony here that is preserved and cherished and fostered every time a patron walks in the front door. It's not just a dusty memory of a long-dead past but something which is living.

We do silent films here maybe six times a year. I think it is unique because there is such a long-standing tradition of this. The audiences here are very enthusiastic about silent films because they know that they're experiencing an original film in an original atmosphere visually with the original sound. There's an experience you can have here that you literally can have nowhere else. We have pretty predictably a good segment of the audience that has never been here before and they're completely overwhelmed by the experience. They become Tampa Theatre junkies, and then they have to have their fix. We're happy to provide that.

People ask me about the ghosts here. I tell people they're like coworkers. They're just part of the environment here. There's a magic about this place. Somehow this place has a personality and a mind of its own. There's a set of train tracks outside the building, which is one of the reasons why we have this unique stage house. For some reason, every single time that I've played a silent film here, every time that we get a train going by the building, which is immensely loud, we're always somehow at a scene in the film that it works. Either there's a train in the film, or in the middle of a storm, or the middle of a war, and it's just one of those Tampa Theatre things.

Love Stories

Ken Stein worked as a fundraiser for the historic Paramount Theater in Austin and fell in love with the place. He then became the executive director of the League of Historic American Theatres, where he became familiar with surviving movie palaces including Tampa Theatre. He also met John Bell, who was on the search committee that hired him. Stein provided background on the league's work.

People started abandoning downtowns for the suburbs, so these beautiful movie palaces shuttered. The league was founded in 1976 by a bunch of historic theater operators who didn't want to see any more torn down. How do we make the case for any community group that is trying to save a historic theater? The idea of preserving, restoring, rehabilitating, operating, and making them sustainable is our goal.

People wanting to live in the city center became a thing again. One of the big draws was access to the arts, in particular live performing arts. These historic movie theaters that had either been shuttered or had sort of withered on the vine suddenly were getting a new life. What was so incredible about movie theaters is they could generate a secondary market for all the other businesses downtown. A movie theater brings a large number of people into the downtown space at off hours. Nine to five, your offices are bringing people downtown. These theaters, along with retail that was around them, were bringing people downtown after five o'clock.

Those historic theaters that are large enough to be Broadway touring houses still exist because they can make money. If you don't, then it becomes

As president and CEO of the League of Historic American Theatres, Ken Stein presented John Bell with the Joseph Rosenberg Award for Outstanding Individual Contribution and Tampa Theatre with the Outstanding Historic Theatre Award at the annual conference in 2024. Pictured here (*from left*) are league board chair Becky Hancock, Ken Stein, John Bell, and Ken Shaw of the State Theatre Preservation Society in Boyertown, Pennsylvania. Courtesy of Don Telford. Tampa Theatre.

> "How badly does this community want to save it?" and "What are they going to do to make it sustainable?" At some point, a person or a group of people fell in love with a building and didn't want it to get torn down. That's at the root of most of these historic theater stories. A love story. Right now, the league is working with about four hundred historic theaters, and that number fluctuates from year to year. That's four hundred love stories.
>
> At some point, when it was about to be torn down, somebody who just loved the space said, "No, I can't." Somebody loved the space and moved mountains to make sure it didn't get torn down. In some cases, they put their day job and their life on hold and became a theater operator selling popcorn and begging on street corners raising money to save the space. That has held true of pretty much every historic theater I've walked into. At some point it became a love story and that's why it's still standing. We still lose some of them today.

Circumstance, surroundings, and theater designer John Eberson's genius can influence which theaters survive, Stein said.

> Would the Tampa Theatre in another city still be standing? Or was it something about Tampa that embraced it and continues to embrace Eberson's mad genius?

If you have an Eberson, you're not selling a ticket, you're selling an experience. A non-Eberson theater can't do it as well because he was that good at creating a space that people really could lose themselves in. These more ornate theaters, and in particular these Ebersons, remain popular destinations because of that, because you still walk into them and go, "Wow." The Tampa is an Eberson like no other.

Eberson was ornate. When you walk into the Tampa Theatre, you kind of think maybe he was a mad genius. I have yet to walk into another theater in North America that even remotely resembles the ornateness of the Tampa Theatre. Maybe it was who was asking him to build it and what they were asking for, but that level of ornateness in an Eberson, I haven't seen it again. It's just crazy. I think it's beautiful. A lot of people would think it is gaudy and I can see why.

The Tampa Theatre is an extraordinary space like none I've ever seen before and since. It's almost like he took ten of his designs and crammed them into one space. It doesn't make sense on so many levels starting with its design. The Tampa Theatre is either an extraordinarily beautiful theater, or it's the gaudiest thing you've ever seen. I think it still resonates today because we're not building them like that anymore. I don't know that we could build them like that anymore. From top to bottom it's like, how the hell did this happen?

In short, Stein said,

> The Tampa Theatre should not exist. I always tease John [Bell] about having the smallest stage in the largest theater. The Tampa is extremely unique because it is technically a single-screen movie house with a thousand seats. It just doesn't exist anymore. That is not a business model that should be sustainable. It is really a testament to the space. No one else can do what the Tampa is doing there.

Centennial

It is no exaggeration to say that Tampa Theatre has reached a new pinnacle. It is beloved and supported by the city and community. The quality and quantity of its programming continues to grow while remaining agile. Changing market conditions

Whether hosting a Sunday matinee or a hydration and phone-charging station after a hurricane, Tampa Theatre fosters a sense of belonging. Here, a girl gets free popcorn during a post-hurricane power outage that affected thousands in the storm-devastated area. 2024. Tampa Theatre.

and the fortunes of the economy present frequent challenges that require constant adjustments.

Communications director Witecki said,

> I liken it to the sliders on a mixing board. We've got our first-run movie slider, a classic movie slider, a live show slider, a rental event slider, and depending on market conditions and what's going on, those are all in constant motion. Back in 2007, when the economy was tanking, groups weren't touring, people weren't buying concert tickets. We saw concert activity dry up to almost nothing. There was a year that John [Bell] was saying that we did like four concerts the entire year. But film was going strong. Coming out of the [COVID-19] pandemic, movie production had been shut down for two years. There was kind of a dearth of new film product coming out. So, we had to back off of first-run film a little bit. But classic films were having a resurgence, and we found people willing to come back for those classics. When the tours [of live performers] all started up again after COVID, that exploded, and that's where all those comedians came from. It is a constant movement.

Through experimentation and establishing traditions, programmers have shaped a calendar brimming over with a mix of new sensations and old favorites. In addition to the programming of films and live events, the theater maintains multiple long-running programs that patrons can rely on. Sunday afternoons in February are dedicated to Black Love, stories told by Black filmmakers and diverse casts. Attendees can strut the red carpet at the Hollywood Awards Night watch party, an event previously known as Oscar Night America. In March, fun and fundraising are maximized with WineFest, a celebration of cinema, fine food, and libations. Family Favorites occupy Sunday afternoons in March and April, giving way to Summer Classics, which is going strong after more than thirty years. September features sing-alongs

above David Byrne was burning down the house in 2006. Tampa Theatre.

left John Legend graced the stage in 2005. Tampa Theatre.

When the Tampa Bay Buccaneers released *Prototype: The Legacy of Ronde Barber* in 2023, Tampa Theatre hosted its premiere. Jeff Fay.

John Bell celebrates "Champa Bay," with championship trophies won by local teams the Buccaneers, Lightning, Rays, and Rowdies all in one season. 2020. Courtesy of Jeff Fay.

Jane Goodall appeared at Tampa Theatre in 2023 to speak about her fascination with the natural world and empower people to make a difference. Jeff Fay.

Comedian Atsuko Okatsuka played for laughs in 2024. Jeff Fay.

with lyrics featured at the bottom of the screen to encourage everyone to join in. In October, Halloween hauntings are a specialty, with a full spectral assault of ghost tours, live events, and favorite films of the spookiest season. Thanksgiving marks the beginning of the Holiday Classics series, which kicked off in 1994 with a mix of classics and the indispensable annual screening of *It's a Wonderful Life.* Live events such as concerts, stand-up comedians, and live podcasts keep the calendar lively all year long.

Most remarkably, for the first time in its history, Tampa Theatre has a sense of purpose beyond its restoration, with dreams not only of restoring the old but of expanding the facility and its capabilities. Given its history of living hand to mouth, the audaciousness of the $27 million Second Century Campaign is striking. The campaign began with the buildout of the John T. Taylor Screening Room, which was completed in 2024.

Much of the campaign involves production infrastructure, such as installing the equipment for the filming of live performances. A creative lab would enhance the theater's popular summer film camps and other programs. A new reception space is planned, called The Peacock Room after Eberson's signature stuffed bird. Along with

The theater calendar is full of seasonal fun all year long. Tampa Theatre.

the Taylor Screening Room, these additions will transform Tampa Theatre from an old movie palace into an arts and entertainment complex with more opportunities for programming and community interaction.

Guided by John Bell's steady hand, driven by the wisdom of the board, and empowered by a dedicated team, Tampa Theatre is not an inert artifact. As it reaches its centennial, it feels very much alive. The devotion of the community has made it all possible. And what a journey Tampa Theatre has taken, all without ever moving an inch.

Now a beloved Christmas tradition for many, *It's a Wonderful Life* made its Tampa Theatre premiere in the spring of 1947. *Tampa Tribune.*

AFTERWORD

John Bell, President and CEO

Tampa Theatre's first century was filled with comedy, drama, thrillers, and suspense, not to mention the movies that played on the screen. The theater's own story has had more plot twists than the best Coen Brothers screenplay, and with any luck there will never be an ending.

I have frequently been asked what I think the future holds for the theater's next hundred years. I have hesitated to answer because I believe any attempt to peer far into the future is an act of folly. After all, I was promised flying cars when I was a kid, and here I am, still waiting.

But if the last century offers any clues about the future, we can be certain of one thing: change. The magnitude of change in society, the economy, technology, and the entertainment industry has been incredible, and the pace of change is accelerating at breakneck speed. Socioeconomic conditions today bear little resemblance to those that existed when Tampa Theatre was built.

American movie palaces like Tampa Theatre were built during a specific window in time in the 1920s when, amazingly, the business model of creating magnificently opulent theaters made economic sense. But just a few decades after their glorious opening nights in the 1920s, motion picture palaces found themselves struggling. Dizzying changes in the marketplace, cities, and society began to render the grand movie palace model obsolete. One of John Eberson's greatest atmospheric masterpieces, the 1928 Paradise in Chicago, was demolished just thirty years after it opened.

Within a few years of Tampa Theatre's own grand opening in 1926, the movie palace that was built for silent films and vaudeville suddenly had to adapt to the

Architect John Eberson said that people don't always understand art, but they feel it. Tampa Theatre's energy, cultivated through a century of human experience, must be felt to be appreciated. Tampa Theatre.

new-fangled invention of sound in motion pictures. Not long after that, the theater's team had to adapt with inventive promotions like "Bank Night" just to survive the Great Depression. It's a common misconception that movie theaters thrived during the Depression; they didn't, and in fact some closed because people literally didn't have a dime.

So, if we can glean anything from the past it is that change is certain, and nothing is guaranteed.

However, despite the vast changes we've witnessed and those that are yet to come, several factors make me confident that Tampa Theatre's second century will be even brighter and more brilliant than its first. Some of my reasons for optimism are hopelessly romantic, while others are quite dry.

First and foremost, the theater itself is a breathtakingly beautiful building that rightly deserves the accolades and acclaim it has received. It is indisputably one of the world's finest examples of movie palace architecture and is regarded as the best example of John Eberson's atmospheric genius. But beauty alone doesn't guarantee a building's survival. People do.

I believe that in an ever-changing world, people are drawn to places that represent permanence, like anchors that keep a ship on station during turbulent weather. Many people view their places of worship this way, while others have special, personal havens that represent something meaningful to them. Tampa Theatre simply feels timeless and offers refuge for those seeking not just entertainment and escape, but solace and comfort.

I also know that for as long as we have walked this earth, human beings have been attracted to beauty, color, and light. We seek out beautiful places, whether those that developed naturally in the world at large or those that are triumphs of the human imagination. We know that our moods are highly influenced by colors, which is why John Eberson carefully curated a precise palette for his painters. Tampa Theatre's atmospheric lighting envelops us with a mystical aura, while the light from the projectors cast precious images onto the screen that often become indelible memories we take with us forever.

An equally important but far less colorful reason for my confidence in Tampa Theatre's future is that the theater is no longer endangered by the need to make a buck for anyone. After its rescue in the 1970s, Tampa Theatre evolved into a non-profit organization, allowing it to internalize the value it creates. Any excess revenue is plowed back in the theater and the organization. The theater's board members

To Tampa native Daniel Cura, Tampa Theatre embodies the essence of his hometown. He had the blade sign tattooed as a tribute. 2024. Jeff Fay.

are donors, not investors, although their donations are most definitely investments in the future of our community.

This nonprofit model removes shareholders from the corporate equation, but of course the numbers still have to add up. After all, nonprofit organizations can go bankrupt, too. With the community's support, we have learned that the theater can operate successfully and pay the bills. But what is clear is that the theater cannot possibly post enough profits through normal operation to fully address the maintenance and upkeep of such a big, elaborate, and complex landmark.

That is why the theater's focus is now on building an endowment as a long-term dedicated source of funds for the upkeep of Tampa Theatre and to ensure that its programming remains relevant to an ever-changing zeitgeist. I like to think of Tampa Theatre as a ridiculously exotic picture frame. You might be able to get someone to come look at a really fancy picture frame once, but to keep them coming back, the content inside of that frame has to be constantly refreshed with interesting and compelling art.

Challenges for future management will be many, I am sure. Today, Tampa Theatre's films and live events compete with an endless array of options for people to be entertained. For a while now, you have been able to watch a movie on your smartphone, which is amazing in its ability to spread the art form across the planet but sad when you think of the diminished experience that a viewer actually receives and the devaluing of the work of all the artists and creative people who brought it to life. Streaming platforms abound, and so it's harder and harder to get people off their couches and venture out into the world to be entertained.

For those reasons, I am far more concerned about the future of commercial cinemas than Tampa Theatre. While I do not wish for its demise, the commercial side of the film exhibition business will likely contract, consolidate, and merge with alarming frequency. It's ironic that the very business model that endangered Tampa Theatre's survival fifty years ago (the multiplex) is now itself facing an existential crisis.

Of course, commercial cinema chains face the same competition that Tampa

Tampa Theatre president and CEO John Bell. Jeff Fay.

Theatre faces, but their failure is more likely simply because going to the multiplex is an utterly mundane experience. There's nothing special about it.

By contrast, there is always a *sense of occasion* when you come to an event at Tampa Theatre. As you approach, the glittering, seven-story marquee heightens your anticipation of what's to come. You are enchanted the moment you enter the lobby and begin making your way past countless antiques into the over-the-top auditorium to find your seats. At Tampa Theatre you immediately know and *feel* that you are in a special place that is timeless, one that has entertained and enthralled millions before you. Your experience is total and immersive because it is imbued with a palpable sense of the history and humanity that is embedded within the Tampa Theatre's paint and plaster.

Aside from its beauty, Tampa Theatre's singular business advantage is that it is historic. It is an extremely important advantage. That is why we have insisted on executing the restoration of the public spaces with painstaking authenticity, often at great cost. It is not only the right approach from a historic preservation perspective, but that authenticity is absolutely essential to our current and future success. Authenticity is the crucial ingredient in determining the longevity of any brand, so our standards of preservation have to be high and exacting to maintain our one advantage now and into the future.

Tampa is a wonderfully diverse community with countless different perspectives, but a common element that anchors us and binds us together can be found in the places we have chosen to preserve. There is a long-standing public love affair between the theater and our community, and while I cannot possibly peer into the future to foresee what changes or new trends may bring, I am certain that Tampa Theatre will be loved by everyone it has touched as long as it stands.

That said, we know the future cannot possibly be all rosy. Indeed, the biggest challenge for the theater's future management may be where to park all those flying cars.

ACKNOWLEDGMENTS

Tampa Theatre opened as a silent movie venue and became one that featured talkies, films with sound. This book will unfold in similar fashion, with more voices from the past added to the narrative over time. I am a big believer in the power of oral history and the importance of preserving memories. Working closely with director of marketing and community relations Jill Witecki, box office and operations manager Joey Hager, and president and CEO John Bell, it was an honor to interview more than thirty people who played key roles in the theater over the years. In service of the narrative, I edited extended quotes for brevity and readability. Sadly, there was not room in this book for all of the material gathered from our interview subjects. Whether they were quoted directly or not, their memories have made this project truly special and will be preserved.

For such a storied place, there are surprisingly few written records about Tampa Theatre's first century of history. The research for this book was assisted greatly by the work of Janna Jones, who wrote her dissertation, a scholarly book, and several articles devoted as a whole or in part to Tampa Theatre. Her previous interviews with people who are no longer with us are treasures, and her passion for the theater permeates her work. Tara Schroeder was also a great storehouse of knowledge, stories, and humor.

Special thanks to digital curator Amanda Boczar and oral history coordinator Dahlia Thomas at the University of South Florida Libraries. Their team made full transcripts and recordings available for listening or download at USF Digital Commons, https://digitalcommons.usf.edu/tampa_theatre_ohp/.

It has been a profound honor to write Tampa Theatre's history. Trying to produce something worthy of the place, the occasion, and the people involved has been daunting and deeply rewarding.

SELECTED BIBLIOGRAPHY

For interview audio and transcripts, see Digital Commons, University of South Florida, https://digitalcommons.usf.edu/tampa_theatre_ohp/.

Dean, Susie Kelly. *The Tampa of My Childhood.* Self-published, 1966.

Fox, Jason Tippeconnic. "Palaces on Main Street: Thomas W. Lamb, Rapp and Rapp, John Eberson, and the Development of the American Movie Palace." PhD dissertation, University of Virginia, 2014.

Herzog, Charlotte. "The Movie Palace and the Theatrical Sources of its Architectural Style." *Cinema Journal* 20, no. 2 (Spring 1981): 15–37.

Hoffman, Scott L. *A Theatre History of Marion, Ohio: John Eberson's Palace and Beyond.* History Press, 2015.

Hole, Donna C., and Carol J. White. *Report of the Architectural Review Commission Recommending the Designation of Tampa Theatre and Office Building as a City of Tampa Landmark.* Tampa Architectural Review Commission, 1988.

Jones, Janna. "The Downtown Picture Palace: The Significance of Place, Memory, and Cinema." PhD dissertation, University of South Florida, 1998.

Jones, Janna. "Moving Toward the Picture Palace: The Tampa Theatre Comes to Town." *Sunland Tribune* 29, 2003.

Jones, Janna. *The Southern Movie Palace: Rise, Fall, and Resurrection.* University Press of Florida, 2003.

Kinerk, Michael D., and Dennis Wilhelm. "Dream Palaces: The Motion Picture Playhouse in the Sunshine State." *Journal of Decorative and Propaganda Arts* 23, Florida theme issue (1998): 208–237.

Levin, Steve. "John Eberson Scrapbook." In *Theater Historical Society of America Annual* 27. Chicago Press, 2000.

Miller, John. "The Southern Circuit." *Marquee: The Journal of the Theater Historical Society* 4, no. 2 (1972): 17.

Motion Picture News. "The Atmospheric Theatre: An Interview with John Eberson, Architect." May/June 1926, 42–62.

Myers, Sharon Moreland. *Curtain Up, Light the Lights: A History of Akron Area Theaters, John Eberson's Loew's and More.* Self-published, 2023.

Naylor, David. *American Picture Palaces: The Architecture of Fantasy.* Prentice Hall, 1991.

Preddy, Jane. "Grand Illusions." *American Heritage* 197 (September/October 1990): 114–120.

Preddy, Jane, editor. *Palaces of Dreams: Working Drawings and Photographs, the Movie Theatres of John Eberson.*

Exhibition catalog. Max Protech Gallery, New York, 1990.

Preddy, Jane, and Robert L. B. Tobin. *Palaces of Dreams: The Movie Theatres of John Eberson, Architect, Working Drawings and Photographs.* Exhibition catalog. McNay Art Museum, San Antonio, TX, 1989.

Quenroe, Elroy Elden. "John Eberson in Richmond, Virginia: Architect for the Twenties." PhD dissertation, University of Virginia, 1975.

Schroeder, Tara. "Still Coming Up Rosa." *Theater Organ,* September/October 2001, 38–43.

Stapleford, Richard, and Jane Preddy. *Temples of Illusion: The Atmospheric Theaters of John Eberson.* Exhibition catalog. Bertha and Karl Leubsdorf Gallery, Hunter College 1988.

Valerio, Joseph M. *Movie Palaces: Renaissance and Reuse.* New York: Educational Facilities Laboratories, 1982.

Westfall, L. Glenn. "Hell Harbor's 55th Anniversary." *Sunland Tribune* 10, no. 1, article 5. Available at https://digitalcommons.usf.edu/sunlandtribune/vol10/iss1/5.

Wondra, Keith. *From the Land of Andalusia to the Wheat Fields of Kansas: A History of Wichita's Historic Orpheum Theatre.* CreateSpace, 2011.

Yoklavich, Ann Kathryn. *John Eberson's Theaters in Texas.* Self-published, 1987.

INDEX

Page numbers in *italics* refer to illustrations

The late Andrew T. Huse was a historian and archivist who lived in Tampa, Florida. He was the curator of Florida studies at the University of South Florida Libraries. His other books include *The Cuban Sandwich: A History in Layers* (2022), *From Saloons to Steakhouses: A History of Tampa* (2020), and *The Columbia Restaurant: Celebrating a Century of History, Culture, and Cuisine* (2009), all published by University Press of Florida.